FROM STEM TO STEAM:
Latino Perspectives

Published by Capstone Press, an imprint of Capstone.
1710 Roe Crest Drive, North Mankato, Minnesota 56003
capstonepub.com

Library of Congress Cataloging-in-Publication Data is available on
the Library of Congress website.

ISBN: 9781669084945 (paperback)

Designed by Poburka Design

Image Credits: Shutterstock: vasabi, (lightbulb & graphic elements) front cover
and throughout, Dedraw Studio, (silhouette) front cover and throughout

FROM STEM TO STEAM:
Latino Perspectives

CAPSTONE PRESS
a capstone imprint

Contents

INTRODUCTION

What STEAM Means for Latino Youth

by Tatyana Ali

As a mother, I know that nothing I want my children to accomplish is taught in a vacuum. Corrosive beliefs that innovation and achievement are the property of some and not others are all around us, and we pass those beliefs on to our children when we are not purposeful in our efforts to include all. Latino children, often multilingual, are well practiced in cultural fluency and adaptation. Growing up with immigrant parents, a mother from Panama and a father from Trinidad, I knew that the beliefs, values and expectations were different in my home than they were in the wider American context. I was often told by teachers that Bs and Cs were good enough for me, while in my home nothing short of an A would do. Luckily, my parents and mentors outside of school gave me examples of highly accomplished people from backgrounds similar to my own. In my imagination, I became the inheritor of their great legacies, though I never came across their names in the classroom or in my grade-school textbooks.

Now is the time to change this status quo for our children, especially in STEAM curricula that has become a key path to upward mobility. Entry points to education exist in the classroom, and context is imperative. At a time when our kids get cultural information from so many sources, the absence of cultural fluency in a classroom is louder than ever. Consider how it would feel to rarely hear stories of great mathematicians, scientists, explorers, artists and innovators who share your history. Consider how deafening that silence is for our children and how that plays a part in their self-esteem and ability to work through universal moments of difficulty in their learning. Consider what you can do, as an educator, to teach our children that greatness is their inheritance.

CHAPTER 1

Advancing Student Outcomes One Decision at a Time, Using Science, Technology, Engineering, Arts, and Mathematics (STEAM)

by Rene Sanchez

Introduction

Not a day goes by that one or more of my sons doesn't ask me to solve and then explain my solution to a "would-you-rather" scenario. I am sure you are familiar with the game. First a psychological experiment, then a game show, and now a seemingly omnipresent teenage-boy question posed to anyone around them. Every day as educators, we address the same "would-you-rather" questions for each one of our students for many of our actions at school and even our time out of work. As I lean into this metaphor, it sounds more like an if-then scenario or philosophical causation.

We weigh every action based on experience, data, policy, input from others, and many other variables. These actions range from designing our lesson plans, contacting families, stopping students in the hallway, calling on students with raised hands, and making one million daily decisions. These decisions come after considering the outcomes and consequences of our actions. So, we are playing the percentages to attain the highest outcomes for these individual decisions.

In this era of high-stakes accountability in education, educators must play the percentages to ensure students have the best possible educational outcomes. To some extent, educators must acknowledge the accountability systems that monitor the yearly performance of schools and districts via testing and other measures. To a much greater extent, educators must play the percentages to help students grow into each grade level and to be prepared for whatever waits for them after high school graduation. For some students, the decisions that educators make could result not just in individual student outcomes but in that student's future generations as well.

School can be a challenging place. In the case of Latino students, one must only look at high school graduation rates (Kids Count, 2023), college attendance, matriculation, and graduation rates (Hernandez et al., 2023) to see that it can take much work to succeed in those measures. If schools are to create success for their Latino students, they must do their best to define ways for them to engage and belong within their school environments.

When deciding how best to make decisions or play the percentages for student outcomes, schools that approach their learning environments using STEAM (Science, Technology, Engineering, Arts, and Mathematics) curriculum or opportunities will provide among the best returns for their individual and collective students. STEAM education within schools has the potential to be the generational change for many of our students. STEAM schools have "a curriculum that integrates scientific training with creativity development to promote innovative cognitive skills" (Madden et al., 2013, p. 541). STEAM education has also been defined in two other ways. Aguilera and Ortiz-Revilla first cite Yakman and Lee (2012) to describe STEAM education "as the interpretation of science and technology through engineering and the arts; all based on mathematical elements" (Aguilera & Ortiz-Revilla, 2021, p. 3), and secondly they cite Zamorano-Escalona et al. (2018), who explain it "as the interdisciplinary integration of sciences, technology, engineering, the arts and mathematics for the resolution of the daily life problems of students" (Aguilera & Ortiz-Revilla, 2021, p. 3). If all or even some of these elements are at work within the school's learning environment, schools will:

> [p]rovide a wider learning pathway which allows more students to reach their goals and enjoy their learning experiences, [e]nhance student engagement and understanding, [c]reate opportunities for a wider group of student leaders, [s]trengthen student focus, [i]mprove students' ability to recall knowledge[, and] increase [student] enjoyment (Chapman, 2020).

STEM into STEAM at a Large Comprehensive Urban High School

My connection to STEAM education occurred while I served as the principal of Houston's Cesar E. Chavez High School during its transformation. This chapter describes how a large urban high school can successfully change course and sustain STEAM education. Chavez's success can be replicable when the district and the community provide enough financial and post-secondary resources to recruit, retain, certify, and support the instructors needed to staff the programs.

Cesar E. Chavez High School is located in the southeast corner of the Houston Independent School District (HISD). The student population exceeded 3,000 students, with over 90 percent free and reduced lunch and over 99 percent students from historically marginalized populations.

Chavez High School's journey to becoming a school that offers a STEAM experience for its students began in 2013. Thanks to the HISD being selected for a U.S. Department of Education Race to the Top (RTTT) grant, the district and the campus could reintroduce Science, Technology, Engineering, and Mathematics (STEM) education to the school. The RTTT grant allowed Chavez to provide students with education focused on STEM outcomes. To support this, the school created an academic house system based on career and technology

(CTE) pathway strands. This house system supported students in developing strong relationships with their instructors and helped administrators to monitor their educational and socioemotional outcomes. As the STEM program matured, Chavez added the International Baccalaureate Career Programme (IBCP) to serve the students who struggled to choose between the advanced academics of the IB Diploma Programme (IBDP) and the CTE STEM certificate and licensing programs.

Chavez High School is set in a unique place in Houston. When it opened in 2000, it was architecturally designed to support the smaller learning communities model. Chavez opened as a STEM magnet school that featured environmental science as its focus. It added other STEM pathways such as engineering and health sciences along the way. Geographically, it is close to the Texas Medical Center, NASA, the Port of Houston, and several colleges and universities; it sits across a tributary of Sims Bayou from a contiguous set of five multinational petrochemical companies. One of the petrochemical companies had been a Chavez STEM program partner since the school's opening in 2000. Near the beginning of my tenure as the Chavez High School principal, I met with a Texas Petrochemical Company (TPC) representative. The representative shared that the company was very interested in having more Chavez students work at its nearby site. She shared that many of its personnel were approaching retirement age, and TPC wanted to recruit Chavez students to provide for its neighborhood and help guide the company's future. We discussed the different CTE offerings in the school and how they could be helpful to this request. One thought that she shared made perfect sense to me. In every district adjacent to this southeast corner of HISD, the neighboring district had an associate degree dual enrollment program in process technology with San Jacinto College. Process technology is a hybrid degree where students learn technology, operations, and leadership and eventually lead within the plant environment. The representative wanted to be sure that Chavez students had equal opportunity to be selected for TPC's high-paying jobs, just like students from neighboring districts.

After hearing all this, our school decided on behalf of the students and the company to pursue the process technology associate degree program. This decision was an easy one to make for the benefit of students and their families. It would take several years to implement, while we found the right personnel, district collaborators, and recruitment strategies. We knew that by taking this path, playing these percentages would change students' lives immediately after high school. After concurrently earning a high school diploma and an associate degree in process technology, students would have a job paying $70,000 immediately after graduation. Some students reported making six figures, including overtime, in their second year. Decisions like this can change the trajectory for generations to come.

In 2015, HISD informed our campus and vertical team leadership that our nine schools were to increase the number and types of fine arts available to students within our boundaries. The goal was to create opportunities for our students similar to those offered at some of HISD's fine art magnets and schools with more affluent students. Unlike the RTTT and Perkins grant funds provided to our school, each school would have to share the cost of a fine arts vertical team coordinator and cover the cost of adding fine arts programming and personnel to their schedule. Knowing that our nearly 20,000 students combined would benefit from these opportunities, the principals and I worked to find the money and the personnel in our system to create the fine arts vertical team over time.

Once we found the money and organized the rollout, we knew we could build on the structure and successes already taking place. First, at the high school level, we could add our first jazz band, mariachi band, and film festival, as well as collaborations with the Houston Ballet and Houston Symphony. Second, as a vertical team, we began an annual fine arts festival to celebrate the students, the programs, and their families. Each school would participate by displaying student-created art in our corridors and cafeteria, having students perform dancing, music, samples from plays, or slam poetry, and showing films created for their media courses. Since we had several locations in the building where performances could take place, we treated it like a music festival with multiple stages. Families could stay in one location or travel a short distance to another and watch representatives from the vertical team showcase their talents.

Outcomes of the Changes

Over the next eight years, we transformed a nascent STEM CTE program into a consistently strong program. Within a graduating class of 600 students, the CTE program quickly produced over 100 students who earned certificates in pharmacy tech, certified clinical medical assistant (CCMA), veterinary tech, SolidWorks, emergency medical tech, fire technology, and IBCP. In 2019, Chavez graduated its first process technology associate degree students from San Jacinto College. In 2021, it graduated its first IBCP students.

In the first three years of focusing on fine arts on our campus and vertical team, the number of fine arts programs increased by 250 percent. When we began in 2015–2016, our nine schools had only twenty-two classes and programs. By 2018–2019, we reached fifty-three classes and programs within our schools. By increasing the offerings at each school and within the vertical team, hundreds more students participated in fine arts.

Factors leading to Chavez High School's successes can be found in the business community's belief in the students and the school, the consistency and inclusiveness in campus leadership, and access to financial, academic, and curricular resources. Without all these lessons intersecting simultaneously at Chavez, this urban high school would not have provided its students this number of STEM opportunities. A school or a district must have a shared vision for outcomes that it expects its graduates to attain. Without such a vision, some students will fall through the cracks of the school or district and not achieve the expectations they, their families, the school, or the community hope for them.

Planning for STEAM in schools or districts requires several items to consider and assist in long-range success. First, a north star is needed to guide the way. Setting a vision for the outcomes that the students, school, and community desire is imperative. The shared vision will enable school or district to set interim goals to ensure progress in the long term. It will also allow for short-term wins to celebrate and acknowledge excellence. Finally, it will give a common language to all stakeholders to perpetuate the work necessary to accomplish the outcomes from the shared vision. Second, account for every student in the building, especially those from historically marginalized populations. If they are not involved in an activity related to STEAM—a class, a club, or a competition—they need to be involved in something the school offers. That something within the school will assist them with engagement and belonging, and it will ensure that they attend school regularly and graduate on time. Third, as the shared vision is set, provide necessary resources for teachers, administrators, and students. Whether the resources include professional learning, extra duty pay, additional software, instruments, equipment, paints, internships, concerts, transportation, competitions, cameras, or anything else needed to accomplish the shared vision, administrators must make sure that teachers and students have access to it. Lastly, once the shared vision is created, throughout the implementation process, a school or a district must find and address the barriers that reveal themselves. The barriers could come from people, systems, architecture, technology, beliefs, curriculum, or geography. The barriers need to be removed or reworked to align the work of the school or the district to the shared vision. Barriers can impede or completely derail the progress of the critical STEAM work.

The administrators and the staff could not have achieved Chavez High School's success story without using technology. Our school was fortunate to be part of HISD's pilot for one-to-one laptops. These laptops enabled teachers to be proactive in planning instruction and gave students access to instruction and curriculum at any time of the day. For our students who needed to work, play sports, participate in fine arts, or look after their younger brothers and sisters, the laptops and the learning management system proved essential to their success. Within our engineering and digital media strands, we upgraded the computers' software requirements to provide the best experiences and instruction. Also, the school purchased or was given the machines, tools, cameras, and other technology for both strands to complete the curricular requirements. A second use of technology allowed teachers to implement the Universal Design for Learning (UDL) Framework. All students need different ways to access the curriculum, share their learning, and engage with the course and other students, even in STEM work. While some students can successfully learn using traditional classroom methods, many others need assistance in one of those three components. Finally, technology for teachers cannot be underestimated or undervalued. The core content courses must support STEM education. STEM and core content courses need a way to track student data in academic and behavioral performance. Knowing a student's literacy and numeracy levels, state assessment scores, attendance rate, and other quantifiable variables can help with intervention and enrichment opportunities. When teachers take student data into planning, whether they use Excel, Google Sheets, Tableau, Mesa Ontime, or other analysis or visualization software, they will support more students and are more likely to accomplish the outcomes of the shared vision.

As the CTE, STEM pathways, and fine arts program matured, Chavez had fewer students wanting to drop out of the pathways. Several pathways also became extremely popular and eventually prolific in producing students who graduated with licenses, certificates, and research opportunities. The vet tech program eventually produced nearly 15 vet tech graduates per year. If the school had access to more veterinary offices, it would have quickly produced a dozen more certificates yearly. However, given the number of graduates, this may seem like a little. Remember that Chavez is an urban school with few students living in the country. The number of vet techs produced here were among the highest in all of southeast Texas. But the most popular program by far was the school's pharmacy technology program. Each year, it grew by 10 or 12 students, and each year, with a passing rate of over 95 percent, the graduates passed the CCMA test and the pharmacy tech exams. Eventually, the school certified 32 pharmacy tech graduates in one year (the most for a high school in Texas). In other words, nearly one in 12 graduates saw pharmacy tech as a way to pay for college or to support themselves and their families. A health sciences student team won a coveted research spot on the International Space Station when their project submission was accepted as part of the Student Space Flight Experimental Program (SSEP). The first graduating class, nine combined Chavez High School and San Jacinto College associate degree students, graduated in 2019. Each of the nine who completed the program had a job offer before graduating. The year 2021 saw the first graduating class of IBCP students.

In the fine arts, our outcomes derived from the idea that we wanted to allow students to challenge themselves to perform not only for art's sake but also to perform for audiences and in competitions. Theater, band, and choir students attended local interscholastic performance competitions for the first time in Chavez High School history. Theater advanced to the one-act play playoffs in its second year of competition. The jazz band played in the lobby of the Jones Hall for the Performing Arts before a Houston Symphony performance. Moreover, to loop back to our CTE program, our floral art design program provided student-designed floral arrangements for every formal gathering hosted by the HISD, the Houston East End Chamber, and the Texas Petrochemical Company.

The community and the district noticed these successes. Thanks to the cohesion and coherence the STEAM opportunities brought to the high school, enrollment remained nearly constant during the expansion of STEM and fine arts. In this part of Houston, competition for students from charter schools, neighboring districts, and even other magnet schools is fierce. Moreover, in 2019, my final year as the Chavez principal, the school graduated over 650 students, its largest graduating class before or since. Furthermore, Chavez's state accountability score increased by seven points, the largest increase of any comprehensive high school in HISD.

Conclusion

In closing, I want to return to the metaphor of playing the percentages for students. Then I will extend it further with a physics analogy. First, Margaret J. Wheatley, in her book *Leadership and the New Science: Discovering Order in a Chaotic World,* describes how quantum physics "imagery challenges so many of our basic assumptions, including our understanding of relationships, connectedness, prediction, and control." She also says, "In the quantum world, relationships are not just interesting; to many physicists, they are all there is to reality." All interactions educators undertake with students result from decisions made over time and in the moment. These interactions are the basis for educators' relationships with their students and with one another. These interactions and relationships occur when the educator plays the percentages on student outcomes. The microdecisions that educators make, when strung together over time, become the decisions that the education system makes for the student from pre-kindergarten through twelfth grade. Another way to look at it is that students are the light of the education system. Students exist as both particles and waves. Students are particles in the daily decisions made by teachers and schools. Each educator-student interaction is a plotted point over the graph of the student's PreK–12 experience. These plotted points, decisions, and relationships delineate the wave of the student's experience within the system.

Educators should be aware of this plotted point continuum within the system and offer the highest percentage strategy for students. When they accomplish that, students will be more successful and will therefore need less intervention. When educators utilize strategies like STEAM in their learning environments, students will benefit from educators selecting the higher percentage option for the students' education.

References

Aguilera, D. & Ortiz-Revilla, J. (2021). STEM vs. STEAM education and student creativity: A systematic literature review. *Educ. Sci.* 2021, 11, 331. https://doi.org/10.3390/educsci11070331

Chapman, S. (2020). STEAMing ahead: Using the arts languages to engage students and enhance learning. *Practical Literacy, 25*(2), 17+. https://link-gale-com.ezproxy.indstate.edu/apps/doc/A627277937/AONE?u=indianastateuniv&sid=bookmark-AONE&xid=9101fde1

Hernandez, E. L. & McElrath, K. (2023, May 10). Gains in educational attainment, enrollment in all Hispanic groups, largest among South American population. Census.gov. https://www.census.gov/library/stories/2023/05/significant-educational-strides-young-hispanic-population.html

Kids Count Data Center: Selected Kids Count Indicators for Nation in United States. (n.d.). Educational Attainment of Working Age Population Ages 25 to 64. https://datacenter.aecf.org/data/customreports/1/6295,9537-9538

Madden, M. E., Baxter, M., Beauchamp, H., Bouchard, K., Habermas, D., Huff, M., Ladd, B., Pearon, J., & Plague, G. (2013). Rethinking STEM education: An interdisciplinary steam curriculum. *Procedia Computer Science, Vol. 20*, 541–546. https://doi.org/10.1016/j.procs.2013.09.316

Wheatley, M. (2006). *Leadership and the New Science: Discovering Order in a Chaotic World.* Berrett-Kohler Publishers.

Yakman, G. & Lee, H. (2012). Exploring the exemplary STEAM education in the U.S. as a practical educational framework for Korea. *Journal of the Korean Association for Science Education, 32* (6), 1072–1086. https://doi.org/10.14697/JKASE.2012.32.6.1072

Zamorano-Escalona, T., García-Cartagena, Y., & Reyes-González, D. (2018). Educación para el sujeto del siglo XXI: Principales características del enfoque STEAM des de la mirada educacional. Contextos Estud. Humanid. Cienc. Soc. 41, 1–21.

About the Author

Rene Sanchez is the Chief Operations Officer of the South Bend Community School Corporation. His responsibilities include Human Resources and Transportation. He now serves as a TALAS mentor after completing the TALAS protégé program (Cohort 3). He has also served on the Houston AHSA Board and was its president-elect.

As principal of Houston ISD's 3000+ Chavez High School, his team founded the IB Diploma and Career Programmes, the Process Technology A.A.S program with San Jacinto College and was featured in a book for its culture and use of Universal Design for Learning schoolwide. Chavez was recognized by the OECD for closing the academic gap with affluent schools. In three years, his vertical team increased their fine arts programs by 250 percent.

Originally from the Rio Grande Valley of Texas, Rene has made South Bend a second home, thanks to his University of Notre Dame degree. Rene earned his J.D. from Ohio State, a M.Ed. at UT Austin, where he began his Ed.D., and is currently enrolled at Indiana State to conclude his doctorate.

Rene is beginning his 25th year in education. After many campus roles, he is trying to learn the craft of district leadership to become a superintendent and, eventually, a professor who will coach our future educational leaders.

CHAPTER 2

STEAM and Elementary English Learners

by Juan Córdova

In the fall of 2019, the United States had 5.12 million English learners (ELs), and they could be found in every state. It is estimated that 25 percent of all students will be ELs by 2025. As the number of ELs continues to grow, schools must find ways to reach young learners. Acquiring English provides ELs access to learning in elementary school.

STEAM activities are a means to provide EL students with content and activities that promote learning English through engaging content. STEAM activities tie together research on how to promote EL students' acquisition of English, valuable learning, the curriculum, and the needs of ELs.

Background

Freeman and Freeman suggest that there are four key actions to promoting student success in English learners:

- Engage students in a challenging, theme-based curriculum to develop academic concepts
- Draw on students' background experiences, cultures, and languages

- Organize collaborative activities and scaffold instruction to build students' academic English proficiency
- Create confident students who value school and themselves as learners

Reasons to Use STEM with English Learners

Builds background knowledge. Having students take part in or observe an experiment, engineering challenge, or other STEM activity creates shared background knowledge. It allows all students in a class to have a shared experience to refer back to.

Keeps students engaged. Building, creating, and using technology are all highly engaging activities. They give ESOL students learning reading, writing, listening, and speaking an authentic reason to take part in these language areas. STEM activities allow students to use their hands, and they also give students real-life experiences.

Speaking opportunities. STEM activities lend themselves to group work, and this creates authentic reasons for students to use academic oral language. ELs need many opportunities to speak in the classroom. Participating in whole-class discussions can be intimidating. Taking part in a small-group building task can be much less intimidating.

The connection between STEM and EL success is apparent. The building of background knowledge benefits EL students across all subjects. The engagement that comes from STEM activities provides entry into the group activities that STEM provides. This type of learning increases the exposure of EL students to both academic and social language. The work provides authenticity and real-life experiences. Finally, group work provides oral opportunities for ELs in small groups, a more comfortable environment.

Adding art into STEM activities, creating STEAM activities, broadens how students can access learning and express themselves. This expansion serves all students, but for ELs in particular, it opens new avenues for expression and involvement.

The STEAM approach guides students' interest by combining theoretical knowledge with practical applications that encourage students to find solutions to real-world problems. This type of learning environment allows students to develop their communication, critical thinking, collaboration, and problem-solving skills.

Activities

Salina Elementary School in Michigan uses hands-on activities for EL students. Following are some examples.

LEGO®: All students participate in LEGO® projects such as problem-solving, model projects in different content areas, and robotics. In addition, Salina Elementary participates in a LEGO® League project to prepare students for the First Robotics program that takes place at Salina Intermediate and Edsel Ford High School. The secondary students serve as mentors for the younger students, which helps them to build a cohesive program. During distance learning, when mixed groups were not possible, LEGO® League projects were accomplished through family pods and older siblings mentored younger siblings throughout the process.

Makerspace: Salina offers a variety of maker projects at each grade level for students to demonstrate their learning in nonlinguistic ways. Staff note, "This really offers all students a chance to shine, especially those whose language skills are still developing." Examples of maker projects include making game boards, models of story elements, and the grade three state of Michigan artifact project. Salina also has an after-school Makers Club with a free choice and exploration format. The school had maker kits delivered to homes while students were learning remotely.

One School, One Book: In this project-based program, every student in the school gets the same chapter book, and the entire school reads the book together at home and in the classroom. The classes then integrate bulletin boards, displays, reading, writing, making robots (this year they are reading *The Wild Robot*), art displays, directed drawing, math, and robotics. The staff notes, "Even though we were in the middle of a pandemic and in a hybrid model, the kids read and learned and created with enthusiasm."

A World of English Language Learners lists some ideas and resources that can be used for EL students:

- Preview vocabulary with students before they begin planning and building. This ensures that ELs are able to take part in group discussions with their peers and practice using the new vocabulary.
- Provide graphic organizers that students can use for planning before building.
- While completing a challenge, use graphic organizers to record the steps a group uses to complete an activity.
- After a challenge, use graphic organizers to reflect on a STEM challenge after it has been completed.
- Use sentence frames, such as the following.
    - "First use the _____."
- Review prepositions. If students will be building and you have lower-level ELs, this is an authentic opportunity to practice prepositions. Provide students with a poster or handout to refer to if these are new terms.

Students can use real objects with Preposition and Prepositional Phrase Task Cards, available from TPT.

I created a set of STEM Story Task Cards, available from TPT. Each card has a problem for a fairy tale, fable, or nursery rhyme. Two levels are included: one references the story and the other is more simplistic. Read a children's book and then have students build something out of the book or solve a problem for one of the characters.

STEAM activities provide all students with learning opportunities that enable them to work collaboratively on high-interest activities. For ELs, STEAM activities encourage collaboration, risk-taking, and the opportunity to learn in a setting where their status as an EL does not preclude them from involvement and participation. The social nature of many STEAM activities quickly builds both social and academic language and understanding. These types of activities are limited only by a teacher's imagination and the time to plan.

Resources

First Lego League
https://www.firstlegoleague.org/

Five Powerful Ways to Join Reading and Science
http://teachersareterrific.com/2016/02/five-ways-to-add-reading-to-your.html

One School, One Book
https://readtothem.org/one-school-one-book/

STEAM Storytime with Chicka Chicka Boom Boom
https://preschoolsteam.com/alphabet-preschool-stem-activities/

TPT: Preposition & Prepositional Phrase Task Cards
https://www.teacherspayteachers.com/Product/Preposition-Prepositional
-Phrase-Task-Cards-2204662

TPT: STEM Story Task Cards
https://www.teacherspayteachers.com/Product/STEM-Story-Task-Cards
-4259861?st=9c4a95de7aaec1fedf964208317ceb3f

About the Author

Dr. Juan Córdova serves as assistant superintendent of elementary school education, English language learners, early childhood, federal programs, professional development, and school improvement for the Hazelwood School District. Before moving to Missouri, Dr. Córdova served as the director of academic programs for HMH Education Services in Puerto Rico, providing academic leadership for Focus/Priority Schools and SIG schools. He previously served as the assistant superintendent for curriculum and instruction in Grandview C4, chief learning officer in Anson County Schools, and a principal and administrator.

Dr. Córdova was an English learner when he started kindergarten. His experiences and struggles as an EL student inform and inspire his work with English learners. He has led or supervised English learner programs in each of the districts where he has served. Dr. Córdova continues to work with English language populations and has provided professional development to educators serving English learners.

CHAPTER 3

Not Science Fairs!

by Elizabeth Álvarez, PhD

Introduction

The dreaded science fair. Most find just the word *fair* to be a four-letter word connected to science. Parents, students and teachers have so many feelings regarding science fairs. If done correctly, science fairs become a school staple where students practice and enhance their curiosity, ingenuity, innovation and star power. It is one way we learn about the world around us as we tie the fair into the periodic table of elements. In the end, it dramatically increases brain power.

Science fairs give students agency, authority and identity in their own work while integrating English language arts, mathematics, humanities, arts, technology and of course science. Ask any student or parent about their science fair involvement and they will all tell you in detail what they learned and, more importantly, about the bonding that occurred between a student and a parent.

If science fairs are done from kindergarten on up, the results are that your middle school experiments become in-depth and advanced. Starting early provides the advantage of having a state-of-the-art science fair, forcing even high school fairs to up their game. Schools wear the badge of STEAM School with pride, knowing the work put in early on to provide only the best in science middle school years.

Unfortunately, science fairs have become viewed as time eaters, inconveniences to regular science curriculum and also something teachers view as done by parents rather than students. The key to having a high-quality science curriculum in any school is holding planned science fairs for all levels starting from kindergarten, where the teachers at that level (K–2) do the push of the curriculum as they prepare scholars for their science fair. Sixth- through eighth-grade teachers provide the pull in preparing our scholars for high school and beyond.

Science Safety

When starting to teach science, safety is key. Learning the names of science tools, how to protect yourself with eye gear, gloves and extinguisher, and what materials to use for cleaning up become lifelong learning habits that can save lives, not only as you teach children in the classroom but as they get older. It also provides time to discuss respect for life and being humane as we do projects and experiments. These become lifelong skills that only occur when teaching to prepare for a science fair.

Projects Versus Experiments

There is a distinction between science fair projects and science fair experiments. Unfortunately, many people use them interchangeably. However, they are not the same. Projects are best in the early years, kindergarten through second grade, although still beneficial in all grades and years afterward. Projects explore the wonders of science, the already-studied concepts and theories of science. Energy is high as teachers trust that children must practice using science materials and begin to utilize the science tools just like a scientist for them to truly immerse and transfer learning. Projects are the catalyst in allowing students to organize their thinking into concepts, generalizations, sequences and other patterns and give them space to begin to understand the world around them. These projects help students learn the patterns of nature, which allows us to continually apply, or transfer, these learnings to new objects or events. It is a great way to teach students the importance of questioning, so as they begin a relationship with science, they begin to question the unstudied, the unknown, the what-if that comes later with experiments. Projects are based on how scientists go about finding out (process) to what scientists have found out (product). Scholars begin to heighten their process skills, such as observing, classifying, communicating, measuring, inferring and later experimenting. Both projects and experiments bring kinesthetic learning. Students experience this kind of learning firsthand when they do it themselves and strengthen their process skills and objectivity. They learn how to be without bias as they rely on observations and data that produce the oohs and aahs from students excited about science. In projects, the hypothesis is already set because past trials have gotten the same results. The project is a demonstration for children to begin to refine their generalizations, test probabilities and develop conclusions. The most common project shown on commercials or TV shows is the eruption of a volcano. This project is one that you would see in early elementary years, kindergarten to second grade.

Experiments, on the other hand, require that students delve into compare and contrast. In this case, the process (how scientists go about finding out) is always susceptible to change. There could be new data, which sharpen observations and thinking and cause a different product (what scientists have found out). Scholars begin to understand variables and the controlled environment. The scholars' questioning is crucial during an experiment. They must understand what it is they are trying to understand and how they will change a variable. The scientific method taught during projects and experiments is not only useful during science fairs but throughout life. When the scientific method is done correctly, a scholar sees the transferability in many life experiences as they grow up, from buying a car to dating. As scholars work on their experiments, they find the opportunity to do true research. What do they want to find out? What are they questioning or wondering? This allows scholars to hone in on the variables as they learn why something may or may not occur. Research is crucial to an experiment to allow students to come up with a sound educated guess, the hypothesis. Only when the research has been done can a hypothesis be created. The research and hypothesis inform how students gather their materials and procedures to actually complete the experiment. Math also plays a huge role when they begin to monitor their findings and develop graphs or charts. Both qualitative and quantitative data are crucial as they move to results and conclusions. In the end, scholars conclude whether what they put to the test can be proven or not. As a science teacher knows, this is important for scholars to understand. Science is never right or wrong. Science can change depending on variables and environment. Scientists must always be prepared to go back and see if another tweak is needed to get a different result, and for this reason scientists never say their hypothesis was right or wrong. Science is constantly changing, always proven or unproven.

In preparing to have a sound STEAM program within your school, all grade levels must have an aligned science curriculum so that science fairs are successful. Teachers must all agree on a common language as scholars move through each grade level. Scholars must also be aware that when doing experiments, especially in middle school, they do not need a new experiment every year. This is not how scientists do their work. They perfect it. They do the same kind of work over and over again and they do not give up. This is why parents and teachers become exhausted with science fairs. They are starting from scratch when it is unnecessary. Instead, allow scholars to enhance their past experiments, make them better, ask a different or better question or work on the kinks from what happened before. This allows students to learn career awareness and an appreciation of science. Changing projects or experiments every year only results in scholars becoming fatigued or developing a dislike of science. In reality, science is a subject that brings much value and purpose in everyday life.

Tips for Planning Science Fairs: Kindergarten Through Eighth Grade

6th–8th Grade: Late Fall Science Fair (October to December)
Students will conduct individual experiments. They wear lab coats and receive an introduction to a rubric on how they will be judged. Judges receive training on the rubric, the experiment requirements (a report using the entire scientific method) and the dos and don'ts of judging. Keeping in mind that these children are eleven to thirteen years old,

the goal is to inspire, not crush dreams. Adult judges play a crucial role in science fairs. Although children just meet the judges briefly, they remember the interaction. This is an opportunity for judges to inspire middle schoolers. This fair is also an opportunity for the kindergarten through fifth graders to visit and hear from their older peers as they begin to prepare for their own science fairs.

3rd–5th Grade: Late Winter Science Fair (January to March)
To prepare for their science fair, students have the opportunity to visit the upper grade science fair. Scholars at this age level can do paired or group experiments or projects. Students begin to come up with ideas of the types of experiment they will do as they prepare for middle school. They will refine this experiment for the next three years. It is a great opportunity for middle-grade students to mentor this group, guiding them in their science journey.

K–2nd Grade: Spring Science Fair (April to June)
Teachers can get students excited early in the year to prepare them for their culminating end-of-year science fair. Projects could be completed in groups or as a class. Scholars may also visit the intermediate and upper grade science fairs. In the end, the goal is for older scholars to inspire the peewees.

As we prepare our scholars for the future, we need to consider the teaching that occurs in our science classrooms. Science fairs avoid the isolation of concepts and the drill-and-kill worksheets where other subjects and skills are taught separately. It is no secret that no subject stands alone in the curriculum, and our job as educators is to make connections and provide skills so that scholars begin to connect the dots on their own. Science fairs allow those links to happen more organically. They foster whole learning for scholars. They give scholars the opportunity to apply their skills in each subject within their project or experiment. When this occurs, the school climate and culture become one of collectivism and integration with a solid science curriculum. The magical energy and buzz produced from having science fairs in all grade levels allow parents and community to see the greatness happening within the school building. So, let's say yes to science fairs! They are fun, but more importantly, science fairs produce lifelong learners who love science for years to come.

About the Author

Dr. Elizabeth Álvarez is a bilingual educator with over 15 years of instructional leadership experience, dedicated to fostering growth and achievement among staff, students, and the community. With a PhD in curriculum and instruction, she has effectively developed strategic plans, built strong relationships, and implemented initiatives promoting social-emotional learning and a sense of belonging. Her expertise extends to the superintendent role, where she has successfully consolidated schools, enhanced family engagement, and championed the development of STEAM labs. She taught upper grade science for 13 years before becoming a math and science coach for three years. She was then an assistant principal for two years before becoming principal for six years at a pre-k through eighth grade elementary school. She led the school to level 1+ status while also working as an adjunct professor at Concordia University. She is one of the founders of the Latino Leadership Pipeline, which coaches and supports CPS Latino leaders as they work to become future leaders in education, and she is a past president of Illinois Association of Latino Administrators and Superintendents. Her past role was serving as Network 8 Chief of Schools in Chicago Public Schools supporting 18 schools (predominantly Latino) where she moved schools from the 30th to the 70th percentile in achievement. Dr. Álvarez has received numerous awards for her work and is currently the superintendent of Forest Park District 91. She is the first female, Latina, and person of color to lead the district.

Some past achievements include:

- Awarded Chicago Mayoral Award for Level 1 Principal, 2012 and 2013
- Awarded Independent School Principal Recognition 2015 by Chicago Mayor
- Awarded Chicago's Top 23 Latina Leaders in Philanthropy and Government for 2017 and 2018
- Awarded 2018 Latina Leader Award by Chicago Latino Network

CHAPTER 4

STEAM in the Middle: A Look at Successful STEAM Initiatives in Middle Grades

by Washington B. Collado, PhD

As educators, when we think of the concept of STEAM, I would challenge us to include in the conceptual framework the opportunity to push for equity and access. But how does that really look in middle grades? This chapter will provide practical examples of what STEAM in the middle grades may look like, particularly when we perceive its implementation through the lens of equity and pushing the boundary of all students' potential.

In the implementation of STEAM programs, many schools set artificial margins to include or exclude certain students to fit a notion of how to maximize the rate of student success. This is code for exclusion and perpetuating inequity. I disagree with this practice and challenge educators to create the conditions for more students to be included in the possibilities of high-rigor classes and STEAM opportunities.

Viewed from another angle, the practice of excluding students and being unwilling to invest time, energy, and resources to work toward pushing boundaries to include nontraditional students is a conscious choice. This exclusion is mainly rooted in marginalizing students who may force educators to think outside the traditional box. These exclusionary practices follow a misguided interpretation of a successful program at the expense of the equity of inclusion, leading to the complacency of marginalization. What if schools consciously expand the selection process; include students not traditionally selected, such as English Language Learners and special education; and invest time and resources to work earnestly for the success of those students with a supportive network that includes academic support, family engagement, technology access, extracurricular opportunities, and strong socioemotional support?

In her book, *The Successful Middle School Schedule,* Dr. Ann McCarty-Perez makes the point that when we look at most school organizations' mission and vision statements and core beliefs and align those statements to a purposeful WHY of living up to the language contained in their lofty aspirations, we see possibilities to expand equity by acting toward those goals with deeds. As Juan Bosch, Dominican thinker and leader, said: "Words have the power to explain an action, but words will never replace an action. Thousands of words are incapable of replacing a single action." Essentially, this quote is a call to live up to the tenets of these missions, visions, and core beliefs.

Thinking Outside the Box: Inclusion, Support, and Motivation

As the school year began, excitement was in the air about the school's new Aviation and Aeronautics program. The selection process for this program went the typical route of choosing students who "could handle" the rigorous curriculum. We decided to start the program with one section, but the opportunities it provided quickly became welcome news for all stakeholders: teachers, students, parents, and the community we served. At the semester mark, the opportunity came to open a second section of Aviation and Aeronautics. But this time, the conversation took a different approach based on a challenge I, as school principal, set for the guidance and leadership team. I wanted the second session to be populated with English Language Learners and other nontraditional students.

The normal concerns were expressed, but the concerns were not a reflection of an unwillingness to meet the challenge. The team showed genuine desire to look for solutions to the expressed concerns. This was done in the spirit of equity, as we understood it, and the challenge was nonnegotiable. One nervous teacher came to see me to express his concerns about being able to "motivate" this "type" of student. The answer was simple: create the conditions for learning, believe in their potential, and motivate them accordingly, and the students will rise to the level of the expectation. The students did rise to the level of the expectation. They showed excitement when we brought in pilots and professionals from the aviation industry who mirrored the students' cultural and ethnic backgrounds. We also arranged support from local businesses and organized a visit to the nearby international airport, much to the students' amazement. All students were treated with high regard for their potential, independent of their prior academic challenges. They learned about the industries, visited the cockpits of commercial airliners, and the students saw themselves in a different light: smart, with potential to succeed.

By the end of the year, the students' success rate was equal to that of the first group. Furthermore, the second group of students saw themselves succeeding at a high-rigor program for the first time, which realigned their own doubts of success at this new high academic expectation. It's an automatic win-win. The key to success is to provide students with the right support to create the conditions to shift their mental attitude and approach to one of possibilities.

Science in the Environment: The Butterfly Garden Project

During my first tenure as a principal, there was a drought in South Florida. Water usage was severely limited, and irrigation was either canceled or very controlled. This particular school had two main buildings with a pathway between them. The pathway was at the center, and on each side, it had quadrants covered with grass that needed to be irrigated. Given the water restrictions, this created a problem.

A proactive science teacher in the Earth and Space classes quickly saw this as an opportunity and teamed up with other teachers and students to build a butterfly garden using the curriculum standards. As principal, I was able to provide some startup funds, and the local municipality's park and recreation department also provided support. The group expanded the project beyond the classes and created an environmental club to provide opportunities for non-Earth and Space Science students to join.

Led by the teachers, students were motivated to have fun while learning about environmental science in a way they never imagined. The club was made up of special education students, English Language Learners, and academically high-performing students, as well as students who struggled academically. When the project was being put together, no one knew which students had what classification; they learned and implemented what they learned, and we got to see the true nature of learning and collaboration.

They began by studying the water cycles and plants native to South Florida that attracted caterpillars for monarch and zebra butterflies. They studied the composition of the soil and how much water they needed. The students, led by the teacher, always maintained focus on the goal that the idea was to limit water consumption. The pathway was originally divided into patches of grass or sod. Math students and teachers joined and used math skills to measure the quadrants and determine the volume of mulch needed. The teachers decided to divide students into groups and allowed them to design their own scheme of plant configurations. Furthermore, they had the idea of including art classes, and art students designed multicolored mosaics to be placed strategically between plants.

The students and teachers visited a local park that featured a butterfly garden and enlisted the support of the county's National Wildlife Federation representatives. When the garden was fully designed, funded, and ready for implementation, they made an appointment to meet with the principal, where the students explained the project in their own words and used the appropriate academic terminology, authentically showing what they had learned. I was a very proud principal, indeed. We planned with the teachers for the students to "convince" me of the project by providing me with a full explanation of the importance of conserving water, beautifying the school, and creating practical space for reading and relaxing. I approved.

The project was fully executed with the participation of city officials, students, parents, teachers, and facility service personnel. Even local police officers joined in to have fun with the learning. After the project was completed, the local chapter of the National Wildlife Federation declared the area a protected sanctuary with its appropriate certification and everything. Years later, the butterfly garden is still active, with new ideas to keep it going.

The Power of Motivation

A team of teachers wrote a grant specifically to expand the before- and after-school programs and successfully obtained the funds. Realizing that transportation was an issue, as the school is local in a high-poverty community, they included activity buses in the grant and created depot stops around the poorest sectors of the community the school served.

The funds were sufficient to create various programs: music appreciation, STEAM clubs, robotics, book clubs, leadership development clubs, and a cadet club under the lead of the school resource officer. The program was so successful in keeping kids productively active after school that deviant behavior in the community decreased, as reported by the local police department. Many of these programs became so successful that they became part of the master schedule. So, in this case, the extracurricular program scope made a positive impact to the school's curriculum in such a way that the elective track was expanded and became more inclusive of and equitable to nontraditional students. I make this assertion to note that frequently, extracurricular activities and programs are implemented without considering that when students are motivated by interests and the right teacher's approach, these activities can potentially ignite an interest not previously realized. This is true for clubs, academic completions, sports, cultural groups, and more.

How to Expand the Impact of Extracurricular Activities and Expand Inclusion

The potential of extracurricular activities should not be underestimated. With these programs, schools can go off script and provide opportunities of all kinds for students to explore their interests, for community stakeholders to join up with schools, and for teachers and staff to pursue their own educational initiatives. More importantly, it expands the students' opportunities to engage in fun activities guided by enthusiasm and interest, without the shackling demands of traditional classroom initiatives.

Education approaches can be challenging and unnerving because school systems, albeit with the best of intentions, sometimes get caught up in the philosophy du jour, or flavor of the times, approach. This approach creates cynicism in teachers and school leaders that can be pervasive and risky. E.D. Hirsh Jr. has been a sharp critic of education in the United States and proposed that there is a set of knowledge that would be instrumental for students to thrive in and out of school. In a book poignantly titled *The Schools We Need and Why We Don't Have Them* (1999), Hirsch continues with another set of critical ideas worthy of being considered. He makes the point that educational communities get mired in "terminological polarizations and intellectual caricature" (p. 8).

If we do not decipher or clearly explain what these terms mean, the lack of clarity may be an excuse used as a rationale for maintaining the intellectual status quo. For instance, the following rhetorical pairings play out in the American educational landscape:

- Traditional vs. Modern
- Verbal vs. Hands-on
- Premature vs. Developmentally Appropriate
- Fragmented vs. Integrated
- Boring vs. Interesting
- Lockstep vs. Individualized

Enhancing Extracurricular Opportunities

When considering extracurricular activities, think of programs and interests expressed by students and teachers and interests or needs in the community, and consider programs that may enhance students' interests or potential as they move to the next level. The following section will provide examples of extracurricular activities.

Sports & Socioemotional Supportive Activities

Frequently, schools may engage in sports sanctioned or supported by an athletic association. Yet other sports or athletic activities can be pursued in the spirit of teamwork. Or students may practice sports options outside of traditional competition simply for the fun of the sport: bowling, golf, handball, fishing, walking or jogging, yoga, and others.

Reading and Writing

Imagine if students were enticed to read just for the fun of it and given opportunities to showcase their creativity by writing essays, poetry, and short stories. Consider a club that empowers students to read for fun and write their own pieces of literature. Now consider collecting those stories and publishing your very own school anthology. These creations can be celebrated as schools look to celebrate literature in activities such as literary weeks or open mic nights when students get to read their poetry and essays for ceremonies or invited guests.

Debate

When students learn how to debate, we open the tremendous potential of igniting their interests in research, seeing another perspective, and metacognitive awareness as they consider how they learn and how to formulate arguments. They also learn to be respectful of opposing ideas and learn how to give credibility to another person's perspective. A debate club is very conducive to field trips of different types, discussion of episodes in history, and the ability to take on poignant and relevant topics of interest to the community, the country, or the world.

Technology

The interest in technology is a vast ocean of possibilities: gaming, robotics, aeronautics, programming or coding, technology support, web design, publishing, music production, film and television production, yearbook design, and so on. A technology club provides an opportunity for students to see computers far beyond their use for social media. Students can problem solve, design or build entire cities, or conduct virtual travel. Again, the possibilities are endless, especially when done as extracurricular activities without the stress of normal classroom activities.

Music and Art

Many schools are an amalgam of cultures, involving traditions and the possibilities of celebrating students' cultural heritage through all types of artistic expression and representation. Students can dabble in the arts in pursuit of their own interests or out of being encouraged by a teacher or a fellow student. Music and art clubs provide students with a venue to engage in contributing to various types of recognition and history-based activities: women's history, Black history, Native American history, and Hispanic heritage, just to name a few. The idea is to allow students to reflect through music and art a rich diversity of rhythms, colors, and cultures that can be used to adorn the school. This is also a great way to expose students to different genres of music and expand their knowledge of the arts. These types of clubs provide a school with great opportunities for the community to enjoy school events.

Environmental Clubs

Environmental clubs are one of my favorites because they lend themselves to leave a mark at the school: butterfly gardens, school beautification projects, bulletin board decorations, Arbor Day celebrations, learning about nature, and learning about the school's surrounding habitat. It's great fun. These types of clubs are conducive to teaming up with local organizations to work on projects.

References

Hirsch, J.D. *The Schools We Need and Why We Don't Have Them*. Anchor, First Edition, 1999.

McCarty-Perez, Ann. *The Successful Middle School Schedule*. Association for Middle-Level Education, 2022.

About the Author

Dr. Washington "Nino" Collado was born in the Dominican Republic in 1962 in a small town called Jánico (HA-Nee-Co). Dr. Collado was raised surrounded by educators. His mother, María Tejada, and seven of his uncles and aunts were teachers. After the death of his mother in 1970, Dr. Collado and his three sisters traveled to the United States to live with their father in 1975. In New York, Dr. Collado began studying in NYC public schools in the seventh grade and went on to Franklin K. Lane High School in Brooklyn, NY.

Dr. W. B. Collado is a lifelong learner and has obtained several college degrees:

- Doctorate in Educational Leadership from Florida Atlantic University, 2018
- Educational Specialist from Florida International University, 2002
- Master's in Educational Leadership from Florida Atlantic University, 1999
- Master's and Bachelor's Degrees in Spanish from Queens College of the City University of New York, in 1986 and 1990

Dr. Collado began his career in education in 1986 in New York City Public Schools, where he taught Spanish and English as a Second Language. In 1992, he and his family moved to Florida, and he continued teaching at Miami-Dade Public Schools. In 1998, he moved to Broward County Public Schools' Multicultural Department to write curriculum and conduct trainings for teachers and administrators on the contributions of Latinos, African Americans, and women throughout the history of the United States.

Dr. Collado began his career in school administration as an assistant principal at Broward County Public Schools and was promoted to principal in 2005. He has served 17 years as principal at the middle and high school levels and past president of the Broward Principals and Assistants Association (BPAA).

In February 2021, Dr. Nino Collado received the distinction of Principal of the Year for Broward County Public Schools, the nation's sixth largest school district. Dr. Collado is also an adjunct professor at Florida Atlantic University, teaching courses on educational leadership.

Throughout his career, Dr. Collado has devoted much of his time to teaching and orienting and has traveled to various countries and over 20 states as a motivational speaker on matters of school leadership and family engagement. He has also served as panelist at CNN Español, NPR (New York), Telemundo, Univision, and others. He has written over 100 articles for newspapers and magazines, including the *Miami Herald,* and has published four books:

- *Parents, Don't Forget your Homework,* 2009
- *Padres, no olviden su tarea,* 2004
- *Liderazgo y escuelas efectivas,* 2014
- *Beyond Conversations About Race,* June 2021

Dr. Collado has received several honors and recognitions for his work in schools and communities. He has been married to Carmen R. Collado for over 35 years, and together they are proud parents of four boys: Mario, Alejandro, Miguel, and Victor.

CHAPTER 5

Reconnecting Roots: The Importance of STEAM Education for Latino High School Students

by Dr. Christopher Bonn

Introduction

Latinos have a rich history of innovation and creativity, evident in their globally recognized artwork and remarkable engineering feats. Their contributions span various fields, from the arts to engineering, mathematics, medicine, astronomy, technology, and agriculture.

Echoes of Ancient Innovations

The ancient city of Teotihuacán in Mexico, thriving around 100–200 AD, is home to two monumental architectural achievements: the Pyramids of the Sun and the Moon. These structures, particularly the Pyramid of the Sun, are among the largest in the Western Hemisphere. A testament to the engineering prowess of the Teotihuacán civilization, these pyramids continue to intrigue modern researchers with their grandeur and construction precision (Ancient History Encyclopedia, 2020).

The Maya civilization, spanning parts of what is now Mexico, Belize, Guatemala, El Salvador, and Honduras, demonstrated a sophisticated approach to architecture, mathematics, and astronomy. They are credited with one of the earliest uses of zero, which significantly enhanced their mathematical and astronomical precision. This early conceptualization of zero is a foundation stone in mathematics and is essential in modern-day binary code, underscoring the far-reaching implications of their intellectual achievements (Mathigon, n.d.).

Ingenuity Etched in Stone

The Inca Empire, spread across what is now Peru, Bolivia, Ecuador, and Colombia, is renowned for its remarkable engineering skills. The zenith of their architectural prowess is seen in Machu Picchu, a 15th-century city in the Andes mountains. This city was constructed without mortar, a feat made possible by cutting stones so precisely that they fit together tightly without adhesive. This technique, known as ashlar masonry, is a testament to the Incas' advanced understanding of geometry and ability to manipulate natural materials with extraordinary precision (National Geographic, 2020).

The calendars of the Aztec and Maya civilizations represent remarkable accomplishments that intricately melded art, science, mathematics, engineering, astronomy, and technology. Particularly noteworthy is the Maya calendar, often praised for its meticulousness and sophistication. The Maya employed two calendars: the Haab, a 365-day solar calendar divided into 18 months of 20 days each, supplemented by an additional "brief" month of five days, and the Tzolk'in, a 260-day ritual calendar with 20 periods of 13 days. These two calendars would align every 52 years, a period the Maya viewed as a complete life cycle (Smithsonian National Museum of the American Indian, n.d.).

Like the Maya, the Aztecs utilized two calendars. One was a 365-day solar calendar, akin to the Maya Haab, and the other was a 260-day ritual calendar, comparable to the Maya Tzolk'in. The Aztecs, like the Maya, found the alignment of the two calendars every 52 years to be of significance (Smithsonian National Museum of the American Indian, n.d.).

The ability of the Maya and Aztecs to monitor such elaborate cycles attests to their advanced comprehension of astronomy and mathematics. They could predict solar and lunar eclipses, and their calendars were remarkably precise (Smithsonian National Museum of the American Indian, n.d.).

The calendar systems were also deeply intertwined with their religious beliefs and social structures. The calendars dictated the timing of religious ceremonies, agricultural activities, and other societal events. The accuracy of these calendars was essential for these societies as it aided them in maintaining order and harmony (Smithsonian National Museum of the American Indian, n.d.).

The designs of the calendars also serve as a testament to their engineering abilities. For instance, the Aztec Sun Stone is a massive carving that portrays the Aztec calendars. It is not merely a functional tool but a work of art (Smithsonian National Museum of the American Indian, n.d.).

The Aztec and Maya calendars are wonders of ancient innovation that integrate multiple fields of knowledge and skills. They are enduring testaments to these civilizations' advanced understanding of the world and their place in it (Smithsonian National Museum of the American Indian, n.d.).

Indigenous tribes, including the Yaqui, Tohono O'odham, Seri, Anasazi, Hohokam, and Pima, had sophisticated knowledge systems that contributed to fields such as agriculture, engineering, astronomy, and medicine. For example, the Hohokam people developed advanced canal systems for irrigation, demonstrating their understanding of engineering and hydrology. The Anasazi (Ancestral Puebloans) are known for their complex multistory architecture and understanding of astronomy, as reflected in the Sun Dagger site at Fajada Butte.

Seeds of Knowledge in the Natural World

Indigenous cultures across Latin America have a long history of medicinal plant use. For instance, the indigenous peoples of the Amazon rainforest have employed various plants for therapeutic purposes for thousands of years. Some of these plants have made their way into modern pharmacopeia, marking a significant contribution to contemporary medicine (ScienceDirect, 2021).

Indigenous cultures in the Americas have also shown innovation in agriculture. The indigenous peoples of Mexico and Central America were among the first to domesticate maize (corn), which is now a critical crop worldwide. This early agricultural innovation sustains billions of people and contributes to global food security (Grobman et al., 2012).

Contemporary Latino Innovators and Their Global Impact

The tradition of innovation in Latino cultures continues with many modern inventions. For example, Guillermo González Camarena of Mexico patented a technology that helped transition televisions from black and white to color in the 1960s. His invention, the Trichromatic Field Sequential System, transmits moving images in red, green, and blue variations, achieving a spectrum of color (Carrillo, 2021).

In seismic technology, Arturo Arias Suárez, a professor from the University of Chile, developed the Arias Intensity method, a formula that assesses the strength of earthquake tremors by measuring their seismic waves. This innovation helps design buildings better equipped to withstand seismic activity (Carrillo, 2021).

The world of cybersecurity was revolutionized by Luis von Ahn from Guatemala, who developed the CAPTCHA and reCAPTCHA systems. These systems help prevent automated spam bots from accessing computer systems and are now nearly universally used (Carrillo, 2021).

In healthcare, Julio Palmaz of Argentina coinvented a balloon-expandable stent, which keeps heart arteries open following angioplasty. This invention has significantly improved the efficacy of angioplasty surgeries and continues to save countless lives (Carrillo, 2021).

Another major healthcare innovation comes from the Mexican American physicist Albert Vinicio Báez, who coinvented the X-ray reflection microscope. This invention has been used to examine living cells and to study galaxies, thus opening up the branch of X-ray optics (Carrillo, 2021).

The chemist Luis Miramontes of Mexico played a crucial role in developing the contraceptive pill. The birth control pill synthesized by his team in 1951 contained norethindrone, a molecule derived from wild Mexican yam. This pill version was soon approved and became an industry standard, marking a significant contribution to reproductive health and family planning worldwide (Carrillo, 2021).

Lastly, Domingo Santo Liotta from Argentina developed the first total artificial heart successfully implanted in a human. This pioneering invention has opened doors for further advancements in heart surgery, saving many lives (Carrillo, 2021).

Future Prospects

The examples above demonstrate the indelible impact of Latino innovations on the world. From the grand pyramids of ancient civilizations to the lifesaving medical technologies of the modern era, Latino inventors and innovators have significantly shaped our understanding of the world and improved the quality of life for countless people. As we move into the future, we can expect further groundbreaking innovations to emerge from this vibrant and diverse community. The dedication to intellectual exploration and problem-solving in Latino cultures promises a prosperous future with transformative ideas and technologies.

Call to Action

To help high school students reconnect with their innovative heritage, it is crucial to incorporate culturally relevant examples and teaching methods in STEAM education. Learning about Latino innovators and their contributions to various fields, students can see themselves as part of a continuing legacy of innovation. This is a call to educators, parents, and students alike to embrace the concept of STEAM education and to recognize the rich history of Latino innovation.

Following are some additional strategies to further engage Latino students in STEAM fields.

Community-Based Instruction: This involves using the local community as a resource for learning. Students can work on projects that address local issues or collaborate with local businesses and organizations on STEAM-related initiatives. For instance, students could work with a local tech company to learn coding or with a local hospital to learn about medical technology.

Field Trips and Virtual Tours: Visit local businesses, universities, and research institutions to expose students to real-world applications of STEAM. Virtual tours and interactions can be a great alternative if physical visits are not feasible. This could include virtual reality experiences, online tours, or live Q&A sessions with professionals in the field.

Recruiting More Latino Teachers: Increase efforts to recruit more Latino teachers and education professionals in STEAM fields. This provides Latino students with role models they can identify with and brings diverse perspectives to the classroom.

Financial Incentives: Offer scholarships, grants, and other financial incentives for Latino students to pursue STEAM education and careers. This could include college or university scholarships, workforce certification program grants, or financial support for internships and work experience placements.

Dual Enrollment and Concurrent Enrollment Programs: These programs allow high school students to take college-level courses and earn college credits while still in high school. Offering these programs in STEAM fields, we can give students a head start on their college education and career.

Internships and Industry Partnerships: Establish partnerships with local businesses and organizations in STEAM fields to provide students with internships and work experience opportunities. This gives students hands-on experience in the field and helps them build connections with potential employers.

Teacher Education and Professional Development: Provide opportunities for teachers to continue their education and professional development in STEAM fields. This could include workshops, conferences, or advanced degree programs. Teachers who are knowledgeable and passionate about STEAM can inspire the same passion in their students.

Implementing these strategies, we can engage and inspire Latino students in STEAM fields and provide them with the support and opportunities they need to succeed. This is crucial to increasing diversity in STEAM fields and fostering a more inclusive and innovative future.

The Significance of Career and Technical Education, Labs, and Project-Based Learning

Career and Technical Education (CTE) programs, workforce development initiatives, labs, and project-based learning are crucial in growing Latino students' interest and participation in STEAM education and professions. These approaches offer numerous benefits by being engaging, motivating, realistic, rigorous, relevant, meaningful, manageable, and measurable. They provide hands-on, practical opportunities for students to explore STEAM disciplines, demonstrating that STEAM is embedded in every aspect of our lives.

CTE programs offer specialized courses and training that align with the workforce's needs, preparing students for careers in STEAM professions. These programs often integrate academic knowledge with technical skills, providing students with a well-rounded education that can lead to high-demand, well-paying jobs. Through CTE programs, Latino students can gain practical experience and develop the skills necessary to excel in STEAM professions.

Workforce development initiatives aim to bridge the gap between education and industry needs by providing students real-world experiences and connections to the professional world. These initiatives often involve partnerships with local businesses, allowing students to engage in internships, apprenticeships, or cooperative education opportunities. Working directly with industry professionals, Latino students can gain valuable insights into the STEAM workforce and develop the skills and competencies needed to succeed.

Labs and project-based learning offer an immersive and interactive approach to STEAM education. Students are actively involved in hands-on projects that require problem-solving, critical thinking, collaboration, and creativity. Through these experiences, Latino students can see the direct application of science, math, technology, engineering, and art in solving real-world challenges. Labs and project-based learning make STEAM education more engaging and motivating and cultivate essential skills highly valued in STEAM professions.

The integration of STEAM into everyday life is often overlooked, but it is essential to recognize its significance. Social media platforms, for example, rely on coding, algorithms, and data analysis, demonstrating the intersection of technology, engineering, and art in creating and managing digital platforms. In our increasingly digital and data-driven world, understanding the underlying principles of STEAM disciplines is crucial for navigating and succeeding in various industries.

CTE programs, workforce development initiatives, labs, and project-based learning provide valuable opportunities for Latino students to engage with STEAM education and professions. These approaches are engaging, motivating, realistic, rigorous, relevant, meaningful, manageable, and measurable. They highlight the pervasive nature of science, math, technology, engineering, and art in our everyday lives. Implementing these strategies, we can empower Latino students to pursue and excel in STEAM fields, fostering a diverse and innovative workforce.

Empowering the Future: Recruiting Latino Students for a STEAM Revolution

The need for diverse perspectives and talents in the subject areas of science, technology, engineering, arts, and mathematics has never been more critical in today's rapidly advancing world. To address the complex challenges of our time and drive innovation, it is paramount that we actively recruit more Latino students into STEAM education, classes, and professions. Nurturing their potential and providing equitable opportunities, we can unlock many benefits for the students and our global society.

Cultivating a Strong Foundation in STEAM

Latinos have a rich heritage deeply rooted in STEAM disciplines. From ancient civilizations like the Maya and Aztecs, who made remarkable advancements in astronomy and engineering, to the modern contributions of Latino innovators in various scientific and technological fields, the legacy of Latino expertise is undeniable. Harnessing this historical connection, we can inspire a new generation of Latino students to embrace their innate talents and pursue careers in STEAM.

Expanding the Talent Pool

Recruiting more Latino students in STEAM education and professions is not only a matter of diversity and representation but also an urgent necessity. As our society faces complex global challenges, we need a diverse pool of scientists, doctors, medical professionals, engineers, mathematicians, and problem solvers who can collaborate across cultures and perspectives. Latino students bring unique insights, diverse experiences, and valuable bilingual abilities that can enrich the STEAM workforce and contribute to innovative solutions.

Addressing Workforce Demands

The demand for STEAM professionals is rapidly growing across various industries. By actively recruiting and supporting Latino students in STEAM fields, we can address this demand and bridge the existing skills gap. Latino students are naturally adept at meeting the workforce's needs due to their strong STEAM lineage and ability to adapt to evolving technologies. Equipping them with the necessary skills and opportunities, we can empower them to excel in high-demand professions, driving economic growth and prosperity.

Fostering Innovation and Breakthroughs

Innovation thrives in diverse environments that embrace different perspectives and experiences. Increasing the representation of Latino students in STEAM, we create an inclusive ecosystem that fosters creativity, collaboration, and groundbreaking discoveries. Latino students' unique cultural backgrounds and diverse problem-solving approaches can ignite innovation and lead to novel breakthroughs in fields such as artificial intelligence, biotechnology, renewable energy, and beyond.

Cultural and Social Benefits

Many Latino students' bilingualism and multicultural backgrounds provide significant cultural and social advantages. In an interconnected world, their ability to bridge different communities, communicate across languages, and navigate diverse cultures becomes invaluable. Encouraging Latino students to pursue STEAM education and careers, we cultivate future leaders who can contribute to global dialogue, foster inclusivity, and address the unique needs of diverse populations.

Recruiting more Latino students in STEAM education, classes, and professions is not only a matter of equity and representation but also an essential step toward addressing global challenges, fostering innovation, and driving societal progress. Providing equitable opportunities, promoting diverse perspectives, and celebrating the rich heritage of Latino contributions in STEAM, we can empower the next generation of Latino scientists, doctors, engineers, mathematicians, and innovators. Together, we can shape a brighter future for all.

Unlocking the Power of STEAM: Empowering Latino Students in High Schools

As we recognize the importance of recruiting more Latino students into STEAM education and professions, it is equally crucial for high school principals, school leaders, and educators to take proactive steps in bringing STEAM to life within their institutions. Implementing effective strategies and creating supportive environments, we can empower Latino students to excel in STEAM fields and pave the way for a brighter future. This chapter explores the next steps high school principals, school leaders, and educators can take to foster STEAM engagement and success among Latino students.

Creating a Culturally Responsive STEAM Curriculum

Developing a culturally responsive STEAM curriculum is essential to engage and motivate Latino students. Incorporating culturally relevant examples, real-life scenarios, and community connections can help students see the practical applications of STEAM in their own lives and communities. It is crucial to highlight the contributions of Latino scientists, engineers, artists, and mathematicians throughout history to provide relatable role models and inspire students.

Implementing Project-Based Learning and Authentic Assessments

Project-based learning (PBL) is a powerful instructional approach that fosters student engagement, critical thinking, problem-solving, and collaboration. High school principals and educators can integrate PBL into STEAM classrooms by designing projects that address real-world challenges and allow students to apply their knowledge and skills meaningfully. Authentic assessments, such as portfolio reviews and presentations, allow students to showcase their abilities and reflect on their learning.

Establishing Community Partnerships and Industry Connections

Building strong partnerships with local businesses, industries, and STEAM-related organizations can provide invaluable opportunities for Latino students. High school principals and leaders can collaborate with these partners to offer internships, mentorship programs, and guest speakers. Such partnerships expose students to real-world applications of STEAM and help them develop professional networks and gain practical experiences.

Providing Professional Development for Teachers

Equipping teachers with the necessary knowledge, skills, and resources is critical for effective STEAM instruction. High school principals should prioritize ongoing professional development opportunities focused on STEAM education. These workshops, seminars, and collaborations with experts in the field can enhance teachers' pedagogical strategies, content knowledge, and instructional technology proficiency, enabling them to deliver high-quality STEAM education.

Offering Dual Enrollment and Concurrent Enrollment Programs

Dual enrollment and concurrent enrollment programs allow high school students to earn college credits while still in high school. High school principals and school leaders can collaborate with local colleges and universities to offer STEAM courses aligned with college curriculum standards. These programs expose Latino students to college-level STEAM coursework and provide a smoother transition to higher education.

Establishing STEAM Clubs and Extracurricular Activities

Creating STEAM clubs and extracurricular activities allows students to explore their interests and passions beyond the classroom. High school principals and educators can support the formation of STEAM clubs, where students can engage in hands-on projects, competitions, and creative problem-solving activities. These clubs foster a sense of belonging, camaraderie, and excitement for STEAM among Latino students.

High school principals, school leaders, and educators are vital in empowering Latino students in STEAM education. Creating culturally responsive curricula, implementing project-based learning, establishing community partnerships, providing professional development, offering dual enrollment programs, and encouraging participation in STEAM clubs, we can bring STEAM to life for Latino students. These proactive steps will foster academic success and inspire the next generation of Latino scientists, engineers, artists, and innovators who will shape our world for the better.

Igniting the Flame of STEAM: Empowering Latino Students for a Thriving Future

We have delved into the pressing need to recruit more Latino students in STEAM education and professions, recognizing the immense benefits for individuals, society, and the economy. As we navigate the rapidly evolving landscape of the 21st century, there is a sense of urgency to cultivate a diverse and inclusive STEAM workforce that can address complex challenges and drive innovation. This summary will highlight the key takeaways from our discussion, emphasizing the importance of collaboration, the expansion of resources, and the critical role of business and industry leaders and legislators in shaping a promising future.

Sense of Urgency: The Time Is Now

There is a palpable sense of urgency to close the gap in STEAM representation among Latino students. As the world becomes increasingly driven by science, technology, engineering, arts, and mathematics, we must seize this moment to ensure that every student is included. Unlocking the potential of Latino students in STEAM, we can tap into a vast pool of talent, perspectives, and innovative thinking that will propel our society forward.

Benefits to Students and Society

Empowering Latino students in STEAM education has far-reaching benefits. Providing them with access to high-quality STEAM programs, resources, and opportunities, we equip them with the skills, knowledge, and confidence to pursue fulfilling careers in the fields of their choice. This, in turn, leads to increased representation, diversity, and inclusivity in the STEAM workforce, fostering innovation and breakthroughs that address global challenges and improve the quality of life for all.

Economic Implications

The economic implications of engaging more Latino students in STEAM are substantial. A diverse STEAM workforce drives economic growth, fosters entrepreneurship, and enhances competitiveness in the global marketplace. By nurturing the talents of Latino students in STEAM, we unlock their potential to become the next generation of scientists, engineers, doctors, mathematicians, and entrepreneurs who will contribute to our nation's prosperity and drive groundbreaking solutions.

Engaging Business and Industry Leaders and Legislators

The collaboration of business and industry leaders and legislators is paramount to the success of recruiting and empowering Latino students in STEAM. Involving these stakeholders, we can align STEAM education with the workforce's needs, ensuring that the skills developed in the classroom directly translate into employability and career opportunities. Additionally, legislators are crucial in advocating for equitable resources, funding, and policies that support STEAM education initiatives.

Expanding and Improving Curriculum and Resources

To effectively engage Latino students in STEAM, we must continue to expand and improve our curriculum and resources. This includes integrating culturally responsive practices, relevant and relatable examples, and real-world applications of STEAM concepts. Additionally, leveraging technology, partnerships with industry, and access to mentors and role models can provide students with hands-on experiences and exposure to cutting-edge advancements in STEAM.

Collaboration and Preparation for Life Beyond School

Preparing Latino students for life and professions beyond the walls of our schools necessitates collaboration among educators, school leaders, scholars, and stakeholders from various sectors. This collaboration can include internships, mentorship programs, community partnerships, and dual enrollment opportunities. Connecting classroom learning to real-world experiences, we equip students with the skills, networks, and mindset needed for success in STEAM careers.

Incentivizing and Inspiring Change

Incentivization is crucial to accelerate progress in recruiting and empowering Latino students in STEAM. Scholarships, grants, and financial incentives can encourage Latino students to pursue STEAM education and careers. Additionally, highlighting the accomplishments of Latino STEAM professionals and providing platforms for their stories to be shared can inspire and motivate students, fostering a sense of pride and identity.

In conclusion, the urgency to recruit more Latino students in STEAM education and professions cannot be overstated. The benefits to students, society, and the economy are vast and undeniable. By expanding and improving curriculum and resources, engaging business and industry leaders, and collaborating across sectors, we can create a transformative educational landscape that empowers Latino students to excel in STEAM fields. Through inclusivity, access, and support, we can unlock the full potential of this talented and diverse population, driving innovation, solving global challenges, and shaping a future where everyone can thrive. Together, let us seize this opportunity to ignite the flame of STEAM and build a more equitable and prosperous world for all.

References

Bowler, L., & McMahon, C. (2019). The significance of career and technical education (CTE) in a changing workforce. *Journal of Education and Work, 32*(4), 358–376. https://doi.org/10.1080/13639080.2019.1603993

Carillo, K. J. (October 15, 2021). 7 groundbreaking inventions by Latino innovators. History. https://www.history.com/news/latino-hispanic-inventions

Cartwright, M. (2015, February 17). Teotihuacan. World History Encyclopedia. https://www.ancient.eu/Teotihuacan/

Darling-Hammond, L., & Bransford, J. (Eds.). (2005). *Preparing Teachers for a Changing World: What Teachers Should Learn and Be Able to Do.* Jossey-Bass.

Grobman, A., Salhuana, W., & Sevilla, R. (2012). Races of maize in Peru. Their origins, evolution and classification. https://www.researchgate.net/publication/235912013_Races_of_Maize_in_Peru_Their_Origins_Evolution_and_Classification

Institute for Educational Leadership. (2018). Culturally responsive STEAM education: Creating pathways for Latino and Latina students. https://iel.org/wp-content/uploads/2018/08/IEL_CulturallyResponsiveSTEAM_final_v8.pdf

Mathigon. (n.d.). The Mayan number system. https://mathigon.org/world/Numbers

National Academies of Sciences, Engineering, and Medicine. (2016). Barriers and opportunities for 2-year and 4-year STEM degrees: Systemic change to support students' diverse pathways. National Academies Press.

National Academies of Sciences, Engineering, and Medicine. (2018). English Learners in STEM Subjects: Transforming Classrooms, Schools, and Lives. The National Academies Press. https://doi.org/10.17226/25182

National Association of State Directors of Career Technical Education Consortium. (2017). Workforce development for diverse learners: A comprehensive guide. https://careertech.org/resource/workforce-development-diverse-learners-comprehensive-guide

National Geographic. (2020). Machu Picchu. https://www.nationalgeographic.com/travel/destinations/south-america/peru/machu-picchu/

National Science Foundation. (2017). Broadening Participation in America's STEM workforce: A review of current research and policy. https://doi .org/10.17226/24984

Ong, M., & Wright, C. (2020). Latino representation in STEM: Data, challenges, and opportunities. *Journal of Hispanics in Higher Education, 19*(3), 242–255. https://doi.org/10.1177/1538192720915066

ScienceDirect. (2021). Medicinal plants in the Amazon. https:// www.sciencedirect.com/topics/agricultural-and-biological-sciences /medicinal-plants

Smith, D. G. (2017). *Diversity's Promise for Higher Education: Making It Work*. Johns Hopkins University Press.

Smithsonian National Museum of the American Indian. (n.d.). The Aztec calendar. https://maya.nmai.si.edu/calendar/aztec-calendar-explained

Smithsonian National Museum of the American Indian. (n.d.). The Maya calendar. https://maya.nmai.si.edu/calendar/maya-calendar-explained

U.S. Department of Commerce. (2011). STEM: Good jobs now and for the future. Office of the Chief Economist.

About the Author

Dr. Christopher Bonn has been a part of the educational field for 30 years. He began as an athletic coach, which shaped his career as an educator and educational leader.

Dr. Bonn attained his bachelor of arts in counseling psychology and special education in 1998, which progressed to a master of education in educational leadership and administration in 2004 and culminated with a doctorate in educational leadership in 2011.

Dr. Bonn began his educational leadership career in Tucson, Arizona, in 2005 as an assistant principal and gradually progressed into upper management leadership as a superintendent of school districts in the states of Arizona, California, and, most recently, New Mexico.

Currently, Dr. Bonn is the chief executive officer and superintendent of the Raton Public Schools in New Mexico. As part of his management, he has been charged with turning the district over to an A+ district with high achievement at all grade levels.

In conjunction with managing school districts, Dr. Bonn is also an adjunct professor for Grand Canyon University for the past five years in the College of Education, as well as an advisor for doctoral students in educational leadership and leadership mentoring.

Dr. Bonn is known for his consulting and team building, both in the educational realm and at the corporate business level. His focus is on systems thinking and repairing broken lines of communication and management between groups within an organization. His philosophical approach to systems thinking improves organizations from the core outward by readdressing the needs of the organization and refocusing their goals to improve the results they desire.

CHAPTER 6

Words of Encouragement, Accessibility and Preparation: Opening Doors to Post-Secondary STEAM Education

by Leticia Ordaz

I imagine a world where Latino children in the U.S. are told they can dream and achieve whatever their heart desires. Where we aren't stereotyped or judged because of the color of our skin or our economic background. College is for everyone and so are STEAM careers.

I still hear the words of my high school counselors echo in my head, "A four-year college isn't for you!" Why would someone say that to a straight-A student? Was it because I was entering unchartered territory as the first in my family to leave the grape and tomato fields and pursue a higher education? Despite the lack of support at my school, I went for it and was accepted at California State University, Sacramento. I pursued journalism and became the first in my family to earn a four-year degree. I eventually became a television news anchor for the NBC affiliate at a small television station in Elko, Nevada. More than 20 years later, I continue to share stories with my community, holding public officials accountable, and giving everyone a voice. I love science and exploration but was never told there was a place for me to belong in this career field.

It's every educator's responsibility to not only tell children they can reach for the stars but to show them the way.

As a mother of two young Latino boys and an advocate for higher education, I'm passionate about letting children know they have what it takes to blast off to the moon.

In my children's book, *The Carousel King and the Space Mission*, I encourage children to break barriers and to not let fear get in the way.

In the colorful story, Maxton encourages us to reach for the stars. Through my book, I hope to inspire all children to go for their heart's desires and believe in themselves no matter their backgrounds. May they grow up to be trailblazers in everything they dream of doing.

Numbers show the Latinx community is underrepresented in science and engineering careers. One in four students in the U.S. are Latinx, but according to the Student Research Foundation, they only make up 8 percent of the STEM workforce. As the first person in my family to graduate from college, I want kids to know they can do anything they set their minds to.

This book was inspired by my son Maxton's fascination with carousels, the moon, and Jupiter. It showcases a young boy who discovers his passion for building and creating. By overcoming his fears, and with plenty of determination and encouragement, he blasts off into space in the rocket his little brother assembles. I have encouraged my sons to see the endless possibilities in life. We need to encourage all children to dream big and let their imaginations run wild. You never know, Maxton could one day find a way to explore the biggest planet in our solar system.

Children will hear many noes in life, but the lesson here is to turn a no into an eventual yes. At just nine years old, Maxton wrote to the Downtown Sacramento Partnership, suggesting they bring a carousel to Old Sacramento to help revive the city's historic landmark. Months later, his wish came true: he and his brother, Bronx, got to be some of the first riders on the new Old Sacramento Carousel. Now, families visit from all over the world and enjoy some adventure because of a little boy's vision.

As a journalist and author, I visit high school and college campuses and interact with young Latinos, who continue to share stories of how they have been discouraged throughout their school life.

When I visited the Migrant Program (CAMP) at Sacramento State, one student shared that he had told his high school counselor he wanted to be a mechanical engineer. The counselor laughed at him and said it was more realistic for him to become a car mechanic.

Some youth will fight the norm, but others will believe the nonsense they are told.

I'm happy this young man didn't listen to the bad advice and instead decided to major in engineering at Sacramento State.

I'm here to advocate for the students who face barriers in life and are easily discouraged. As the first person in my family to graduate from college, I want kids to know they are smart and can do anything they set their mind to.

Imagine if more kids were told they could be doctors, engineers, scientists, mathematicians, or paleontologists. Our world would be a better place.

I'm hopeful that Latinx educators are uniting to make change. Through my own work promoting STEAM through children's books in the classroom and at community events, I see big brown eyes light up. I hear little voices say, "That brown astronaut on the cover of your book is me! I will go to the moon one day."

What will college campuses across the country look like when we make them accessible to everyone?

What will you do to make sure our youth have the confidence and preparation to have a brighter future?

Educators, set up those college tours and get all the kids in elementary school to start thinking about college, especially those in marginalized communities.

The world will be a better place when we decide to invest and believe in our young scholars, no matter the color of their skin or where they come from.

Latinx deserve to see themselves in positions that go beyond the service industry.

Let's give them the tools to blast off into space and reach their true potential.

About the Author

Leticia Ordaz is the founder of bilingual publishing house Cielito Lindo Books and an award-winning children's book author at the International Latino Book Awards. She is also an Emmy-nominated anchor/reporter in Sacramento, California. Leticia is the author of *The Adventures of Mr. Macaw, That Girl on TV Could Be Me! The Journey of a Latina News Anchor, Mr. Macaw's Paleta Adventure*, and *The Carousel King and the Space Mission*. As a literacy ambassador, she is excited to share bilingual stories with children around the world. Leticia hopes to break barriers and change statistics that currently show only 7 percent of children's books feature Latinx characters or subjects, and only 10 percent of authors and illustrators in the U.S. are Latinx.

CHAPTER 7

STEAM Assessment and Accountability

by Elda Garcia, PhD

Assessment and accountability in STEAM education are critical components that ensure students receive an enhanced learning experience that yields expected learning outcomes and the acquisition of the proficiency skills required for academic and career success.

Assessment

The purpose of STEAM assessment, like traditional K–12 assessment, is to measure students' learning and progress. Assessments evaluate the knowledge and skills that students have acquired throughout or at the end of a course or school year. STEAM assessments and programs emphasize a well-rounded education that fosters problem-solving, critical thinking, and creativity. STEAM specifically aims to measure learning related to its core program areas of science, technology, engineering, arts, and mathematics, while demonstrating their skills and creativity. STEAM assessments often require students to apply their knowledge to real-world situations and arrive at innovative solutions, like the higher-order thinking built into revised versions of state summative assessments.

Assessment in STEAM and traditional education may include standardized assessments such as ACT and SAT; formative assessments, which are ongoing assessments that provide feedback to students and teachers about progress toward learning goals; and summative assessments, which evaluate student learning at the end of a unit, course, or program. STEAM assessment approaches of pre/post-test, peer review, self-assessment, and performance-based assessments, such as projects, portfolios, or presentations, are distinct from traditional approaches to assessments. The skills that STEAM programs build and their approach to assessment challenge traditional assessment methodologies to evolve.

Benefits of STEAM

Existing evidence suggests that STEAM education can be a valuable framework for promoting deeper learning and improving assessment performance. There is evidence to suggest that incorporating elements of STEAM education can improve the overall learning experience and assessment performance. Here are a few ways that STEAM can positively impact student learning and assessment:

- **STEAM education promotes creativity and critical thinking.** By incorporating art and design into STEM subjects, STEAM education encourages students to approach problems in new and creative ways. This can lead to deeper understanding and better performance on assessments (Hidi & Renninger, 2006).

- **Technology-based assessment tools can facilitate assessment.** Technology-based assessment tools can provide immediate feedback to students and allow educators to track progress over time. This can help identify intervention areas and the alignment of additional support and personalized instruction. These tools can also improve student engagement and motivation, leading to better performance on assessments (Chen, Chang, & Wang, 2018).

- **Hands-on learning can improve retention.** STEAM education often involves hands-on, experiential learning, which can help students retain information better than passive forms of learning (Windschitl, Thompson, & Braaten, 2008).

- **STEAM education promotes interdisciplinary learning.**
  By incorporating multiple subjects into a single lesson, STEAM education can help students make connections between different areas of knowledge. This can improve their ability to apply what they've learned on assessments.

Overall, STEAM education may not be the silver bullet that improves assessment performance, but it can certainly provide a valuable framework for engaging students and promoting deeper learning and skill enhancement.

Accountability

Accountability in education is often based on standardized test scores, student progress, graduation rates, and college enrollment rates. Additionally, schools are held accountable for ensuring that underrepresented groups, such as poor and minority students, are being educated equally and fairly and are not being disproportionately impacted by achievement gaps. Less frequently, some accountability systems include feedback from students, parents, and educators.

STEAM programs may also be held accountable for ensuring that girls are given equal opportunities to participate in STEAM education. To promote accountability in STEAM education, schools and policymakers may establish specific benchmarks and goals for student achievement, and they may provide resources and support to help schools meet these goals. Ultimately, effective assessment and accountability practices in STEAM education can help ensure that students are prepared for the challenges and opportunities of the modern workforce.

The Punitive Nature of Accountability

To date, assessment and accountability have been used punitively, rather than transformatively. Schools, teachers, and students have been penalized for low test scores without consideration for challenge or circumstance (Braun, 2016). To arrive at transformative rather than punitive accountability systems, the assessment industry must acknowledge and address the history of power and privilege in education and assessment and implement inclusivity at all levels and within all outcomes. This requires a commitment to the diversification and representation of people of color within the education and assessment fields by prioritizing recruitment, inclusion, and training of educators and psychometricians from diverse cultural and racial backgrounds, people of color who could support and expedite the development of culturally relevant curriculum and assessments.

Equity and Fairness

The education system and its assessments have been challenged by issues of equity, fairness, and social justice. Although issues of diversity, equity, and inclusion are not new, they have gained incredible momentum in recent years. The result has been reinvigorated advocacy for our students of color, poverty, and special needs (Randall, 2021).

Post-pandemic data has reaffirmed concerns around achievement gaps between historically marginalized students and their peers (National Center for Education Statistics (2022). This was a well-known and well-documented pre-pandemic fact that has fueled advocates to share recommendations for detecting racism and inequities in our assessments and pursue solutions for ensuring fairness in the assessment systems that govern them.

Advocating for sensible assessments, policies, and procedures is especially hard and it takes time, effort, and a plan. More than that, it takes intention and focus. An improved system would include a fair social justice framework, updated technical capabilities, frequent and remote testing abilities, testing tools for parents to evaluate their child's grade level status, and solutions for children who may be at a deficit or regressing. This will require acknowledgement, intention, commitment, training, and evaluation of ourselves, our assessments, our policies, and our systems. A communication plan, transparency, support, and resources are key (D' Brot, 2017).

Collaboration and Partnerships

The pandemic sparked a refreshing era of collaboration and partnership. It opened opportunities for organizations who historically advocated in silos to break down barriers and come together in the spirit of partnership to work toward the common goals of achieving fair, equitable, and high-quality curriculum and instruction, assessments, and accountability systems. The collaboration resulted in a newly discovered understanding of the greatest challenges among the assessment community and prepared stakeholders for addressing and overcoming them. The process and outcomes are topics for another time, but the key priorities and key steps to the collaboration process are worthy of noting.

Priorities

- High-quality assessment systems based on state standards
- Common high-quality curricula
- Individualized assessments that increase personalized learning and learner-centered pedagogical approaches
- Non-test-based measures of progress
- Improved use of assessment data
- Understand the pandemic impact on testing policy, equity, and fairness for students with disabilities and English learners
- Funding challenges
- Future of accountability
- Navigating the politics

Process

- Scheduled, targeted, and intentional discussions about the most significant deficits
- Explore tangible and attainable solutions
- Organized approach and plan of action
- Focus groups who identify specific needs and work groups who assess impact and propose recommendations
- Obtain feedback from the field
- Implementation and adjustment period
- Diverse and comprehensive review of the findings

Supporting good local practice of comprehensive and holistic assessment systems that drive learning forward for all students is of the utmost importance. So is having a theory of action that includes a reflection on what is happening in schools, owning past failures, extracting lessons learned, and applying them to the work toward solutions that create an assessment system superior to any that have preceded it (Marion, 2010). Today's goals are meaningful, well-researched and thought-out, actionable solutions that create an assessment system of which all stakeholders can be proud.

The collaboration must continue with a concrete call to action that holds up accountability in a positive way and results in fair and equitable assessment practices that support our most heavily impacted Latino, Black, and marginalized students.

Reimagining Assessments

The pandemic and social justice issues jarred the face of education and assessment. Initial chaos was followed by profound support and leadership. Still, most of our students were negatively impacted socially, emotionally, and academically, due to the disruption of our educational system. Most heavily impacted were our Latino, Black, and marginalized students. Digital access and inequities in our current system caused a great deal of concern, raising questions about how we would assess students effectively, and more importantly, about the effectiveness of our current assessments altogether.

Advocates of assessments and equity call for a redefined purpose for assessment with a common vision. The call is for a comprehensive assessment system based on input from all major stakeholders and moves beyond administering assessments and compliance and toward increasing the value of assessments.

References

Braun, H. (2016). *Meeting the Challenges to Measurement in an Era of Accountability*. Routledge.

Chen, C. H., Chang, C. C., & Wang, K. T. (2018). The effect of technology -based assessment on students' engagement and motivation in science learning. *Journal of Educational Computing Research, 56*(4), 559-578.

D' Brot, J. (2017). How we talk about results of assessment and accountability systems. *Educational Leadership, 75*(8), 44-49. https://www.nciea.org/blog /how-we-talk-about- results-of-assessment-and-accountability-systems/

Hidi, S., & Renninger, K. A. (2006). The four-phase model of interest development. *Educational Psychologist, 41*(2), 111–127.

Kellaghan & D. L. Stufflebeam (Eds.), *International Handbook of Educational Evaluation* (pp. 515–535). Springer.

Kennedy, C. & Clifton, N. (2019). Instruction for Youth in School and Public Libraries. *Evaluation and Assessment, 42*(1), 1–12.

Marion, S. (2010). Developing a theory of action: A foundation of the NIA response. Center for Assessment. https://www.nciea.org/wp-content /uploads/2021/11/Theory-of-Action_041610_2.pdf

National Center for Education Statistics. (2022). The nation's report card: NAEP long-term trend assessment results: Reading and math. https://www .nationsreportcard.gov/highlights/ltt/2022/

Randall, J. (2021). Moving Towards Justice-Oriented Assessment. Center for Measurement Justice. https://measurementjustice.org/2022/03/justice -oriented-assessment/

Seeber, K. (2013). Using assessment results to reinforce campus partnerships. *College & Undergraduate Libraries, 20*(3–4), 352–365. https://doi-org .libproxy.lib.unc.edu/10.1080/10691316.2013.829366

Sireci, S. G., & Zenisky, A. L. (2006). Equity issues in testing: Theory and practice. In T.

Sireci, S. G. (2021). 6 big changes in standardized tests —including less focus on grading students and more on learning. The Conversation. https://theconversation.com/6-big-changes-in-standardized-tests-including-less-focus-on-grading-students-and-more-on-learning-158289

Sireci, S. G., Scarpati, S. E., & Li, S. (2005). Test accommodations for students with disabilities: An analysis of the interaction hypothesis. *Review of Educational Research 75*(4) pp. 457–490. American Educational Research Association. https://www.jstor.org/stable/3516104

Smith, J., Johnson, K., & Brown, M. (2021). STEAM assessment and accountability: Strategies for measuring learning in science, technology, engineering, arts, and mathematics. *Journal of STEM Education*, 22(3), 35–47.

Windschitl, M., Thompson, J., & Braaten, M. (2008). Beyond the scientific method: Model-based inquiry as a new paradigm of preference for school science investigations. *Science Education, 92*(5), 941–967.

About the Author

Dr. Elda Garcia holds a PhD in counselor education from Texas A&M University–Corpus Christi, Texas. She also earned a BA in psychology/sociology from Texas A&I University and an MS in psychology from Texas A&M–Kingsville, Texas.

She is the executive director for the National Association of Testing Professionals (NATP), where she focuses on the support and empowerment of testing coordinators through a network of peers and resources that streamline assessment efforts at all levels.

Dr. Garcia works to establish and maintain key partnerships across and among school districts, state education agencies, and vendors in each state and across the nation, with the common goal of improving assessments and assessment systems for all students.

In addition to her work at NATP, Dr. Garcia has also served as the president for the Texas Statewide Network of Assessment Professionals

(TSNAP), the largest assessment network in Texas, where she was the first Latinx president. TSNAP, which has over 1,200 members, supports the efforts of testing coordinators while collaborating with the Texas Education Agency, local service centers, and sponsored vendors.

Dr. Garcia served as the director of assessment and accountability for the Corpus Christi Independent School District (CCISD) for almost 20 years. During that time, she oversaw the district's local and state assessment programs, supported campus administrators as they worked toward performance goals, and oversaw the district's state accountability efforts, as well as research and program evaluation efforts. She also participated in assessment working and accessibility groups for the Texas Education Agency to improve policies and practices.

Dr. Garcia has served on the Executive Committee for the Corpus Christi Principals and Supervisors Association. She has presented at professional conferences, including the National Council on Measurement in Education (NCME), National Conference on Student Assessment (NCSA), Association of Latino Administrators and Superintendents (ALAS), Texas Assessment Conference, and numerous state conferences in Texas. She is also a contributing author to *Substance Abuse Counseling, 3rd and 4th Editions*, published by Prentice-Hall, and *The Road to Doctoral Success and Beyond*, published by the *International Journal of Doctoral Studies*. Prior to her work in public education, Dr. Garcia worked in the fields of counseling and medical social work with a focus on marginalized, disadvantaged, and at-risk populations.

CHAPTER 8

How to Fund STEAM

by Nury Castillo Crawford

The context of STEAM has been steadily creeping into our everyday world for about a decade now, and I believe our world of public education has been expecting its full-force impact for some time now. As with many initiatives and innovations, many of the students we serve do not receive the fruits of said labor well past an initiative's due date. Would you agree?

The entire world tells us we need as many bright minds as possible to understand how the world works and how we can make it better. This includes each and every one of our students. STEAM is important and it is necessary. For our global community to reach its full potential, each one of our students must strive to reach theirs, and in the world we live in today, it cannot happen without some background knowledge and experiences that live within the context of a STEAM-related field. It is only through access to STEAM-aligned resources that expand their thinking and experiences that we will we be able to see each of them become a part of the growth and success that is sure to come in science-, technology-, engineering-, arts- and mathematics-focused careers. To maximize these learning opportunities, you will need funding.

Local and national companies are in the areas of engineering, science, healthcare, manufacturing, and related fields. Many auto industries, cell phone makers, and even gasoline fuel companies have grants. Due to the high increase of demand for equity, many of these companies have specific demographic groups, such as female and minority groups, they would like to collaborate with. Also, companies want to make a significant impact, so schools or libraries that have few or no STEM programs are more attractive.

As you are writing your grant, the best advice I can give you is to precisely and clearly follow the instructions of the funder. There is no easier way to not qualify than to deviate from the instructions. You literally open up the opportunity for others, even if their work is not as well organized or put together as yours. Follow the instructions. (I think that's what we tell the kids too.) Other than that, here is a brief list of tips on how to keep your grant alive. You do not need to be an expert at grant writing to get this done.

Determine the need. Specifically explain why you need funding. Your state may have adopted the Next Generation Science Standards, and your curriculum may require alterations to meet these standards. A large number of students may not meet expectations in math or science. Or maybe your district is determined to fill the "opportunity gap" for low-income students and minorities.

Make your goals clear. How will you use the grant? Set realistic goals and strive for results that are measurable. For example: "Through our five-year strategic plan, we will launch a pilot program to integrate science and engineering lessons for grades two through four, adding an average of 150 students per grade in three schools each year, which will reach 1,350 students in three years."

Determine how you will monitor and rate the success of this initiative. How will you know that the introduction of a new curriculum made a change? Higher student test scores? Improved performance after implementation compared to performance before implementation? Be specific when noting what tools you will use to monitor and rate the success of the initiative.

Obtain permission, and keep your leaders or supervisors informed. This step is easy to skip, especially when you've done all your research and you have your eyes set on the prize. But don't forget about it! It would be disheartening to go through all of the steps and then be denied because you do not have the support you need from your leadership team. Most grants require you to show that you have approval from school administrators.

Create a budget. Your budget should clearly reflect an operations budget, as well as consumables, in-kind support, and how much the school district will contribute. Do not forget specific needs such as transportation and an interpreter or translator, who can make calls for you and translate messages to send to parents. It is a positive sign to sponsors when they know you and your initiative have the full support of the district.

Identify potential funders. This is where you can search for national and local funders.

Follow instructions. Each funder will give detailed directions on what they expect from you. Double-check your work after carefully following the instructions. As I shared before, doing this incorrectly is the fastest way for your request to be set aside.

Design a sustainable project plan. Set a realistic vision for the project, gather the community's support by creating an advisory board, and be transparent. In this way, others will join you in promoting and celebrating this initiative.

Begin early. The grant process is quite lengthy, and you will need to have all of your data, budget, and plan in place before you start the application.

Write a great cover letter. Your cover letter is your elevator pitch; it needs to be concise and to the point. Do not overindulge in words. Make your vision clear and clarify how and why their support is an integral variable to ensuring the success of the project and the students it will serve.

In 2019, I launched a mentoring program for Latino youth. The focus since its inception was to help students build their self-esteem. To accomplish this goal, the advisory team and I discussed ways people start to feel good about themselves. We noted variables like background knowledge, pride in oneself, understanding one's own culture and the contributions of said culture within the whole community, and having access to learning opportunities, as well as experiences that help one grow personally and professionally. That is how we came to realize we would focus on STEAM, literacy, and cultural empowerment. In the realm of STEAM, we wanted to expose the students to early coding as well as intermediate coding experiences. Phone calls and emails were sent to one of our local universities in Atlanta, Georgia Tech. We learned that Georgia Tech had an office that supported Latino students who were enrolled or considering enrollment. They in turn connected us with a professor who had written a grant to support Latino K–12 youth in the world of tech. I met with her and quickly learned we had similar aspirations in empowering our youth. That first year that office offered us free coding and continued to do so each year. They extended their reach and support by offering other coding sessions for those who had mastered the beginner coding standards. During our second year of the mentoring program, we connected with the National Hispanic Heritage Foundation. They too have a tech component and were readily open to collaborate and brainstorm on how they could support us remotely. Since coding programming uses electronic devices, it was a seamless process after we registered the students and connected them to the program. We were present at each session, and I would recommend the same for you. While the sessions were great, they were all led by a young adult, who at times may not have been aware of the parameters we know as leaders in education. It is always best to be present throughout the entirety of a program, especially if it is being cohosted by an outside agency. During the summer of our second year, we were able to connect with the Latino BRG group, who ultimately connected us with a department that supported students as a whole. They have been great supporters of the program as well. They have come to our Saturday camps and hosted drone and artificial intelligence sessions.

The wonderful part about these countless other collaborations is that since they were STEAM-related, we were able to continue without skipping a beat during the worldwide COVID-19 pandemic. We created online sign-ups and reminders and held sessions online. Because of the pandemic, we were able to gather the support of these and other community stakeholders to give away over 100 new devices for students to continue their learning.

For me, I have come to learn that if there is a will, there is a way. Connecting with other like-minded leaders is also a great strategy and has helped me continually find support for our students.

With our current status of equity-focused leadership and diversity and inclusion in corporate America, you will find it pleasantly surprising that many corporations have updated their goals and community outreach to include supporting initiatives such as these. Our country's Latino population is increasing. By 2025, one in four K–12 children will be Latino. The success of Latino youth is the success of the United States of America. If the goal is to increase tech in and out of the classroom, you must have a dedicated team to focus on this initiative. It will not be a priority unless you make it one. Our students deserve for us to be intentional and strategic in offering them a glimpse of what awaits them. It is only a glimpse, since the world is changing daily all around us, and we cannot yet imagine what it will look like once they enter the workforce.

About the Author

Nury Castillo Crawford has a positive track record of being a transformational leader in public education. Currently, she is the executive director of alternative education and innovation in the Madison Metropolitan School District, where she leads 16 district-wide programs to ensure youth reach their full potential.

Nury is the owner of 1010 Publishing and the founder of the nonprofit The Little Book Spot: A Multilingual Bookstore. Both entities were created to increase access to literacy and literacy-related resources, with an emphasis in bilingual and biliterate books that reflect biculturalism and pride in ancestry and culture.

Nury has been recognized nationally for her advocacy and leadership. She is a sought-out national speaker in the areas of parent involvement, education, mentoring, equity, and bilingualism. She is also a proud award-winning author of numerous books and continues to present throughout the country, highlighting the role Latinos play in American culture.

CHAPTER 9

The Metaverse in STEAM Schools: Theory, Practice, Sustainability, and Evolution—A Latino Perspective

by Zandra Jo Galván

Greenfield Union School District, Superintendent
California Association of Latino Superintendents and Administrators, President

Embracing the metaverse in STEAM schools from a Latino perspective holds tremendous potential for empowering students, fostering creativity, and promoting inclusivity. By merging technology, education, and cultural representation, we can create immersive and collaborative learning experiences that transcend physical boundaries and inspire the next generation of innovators and leaders. —Zandra Jo Galván

Abstract

This chapter explores the concept of the metaverse and its application in STEAM (Science, Technology, Engineering, Arts, and Mathematics) schools from a Latino perspective. It discusses the theoretical foundations of the metaverse, its practical implementation in educational settings, and its potential for sustainability and evolution. Additionally, this chapter highlights examples of how both the United States and Latin American countries have played a leading role in advancing the metaverse in the context of STEAM education. The chapter draws on professional and scholarly citations to provide a comprehensive understanding of the topic.

Introduction

The emergence of the metaverse has sparked significant interest and excitement in the fields of education and technology. It presents a new frontier for immersive and interactive experiences, revolutionizing the way we learn, collaborate, and create. This chapter delves into the metaverse's role within the context of STEAM schools, focusing on the theory, practice, sustainability, and evolution of this concept from a Latino perspective. By examining examples from both the United States and Latin American countries, we can gain valuable insights into the current landscape and potential future directions for the metaverse in STEAM education.

Embracing the metaverse in STEAM schools from a Latino perspective holds tremendous potential for empowering students, fostering creativity, and promoting inclusivity. The emergence of the metaverse has sparked significant interest and excitement in the fields of education and technology, ushering in a new era of immersive and interactive experiences that have the power to revolutionize the way we learn, collaborate, and create.

In this chapter, we embark on a comprehensive exploration of the metaverse's role within the context of STEAM schools, with a particular focus on its theory, practice, sustainability, and evolution from a Latino perspective. By delving into the theoretical foundations of the metaverse, we can understand its essence as a virtual reality space where users can engage with computer-generated environments and other participants in real time. This combination of augmented reality, virtual reality, and social networking creates a shared immersive experience that holds immense potential for transforming education.

We delve into the practical implementation of the metaverse in STEAM schools, where it serves as a catalyst for hands-on, experiential learning. Through virtual laboratories and simulations, students can engage in scientific experiments and simulations in a safe and controlled environment, enhancing accessibility, scalability, and cost-effectiveness compared with traditional physical labs. Additionally, collaborative design and creation spaces in the metaverse enable students to work together on engineering projects, architectural designs, and artistic collaborations, fostering cross-cultural exchange and promoting diverse perspectives.

Sustainability and evolution are crucial considerations for the metaverse in STEAM education. Addressing issues of infrastructure and accessibility is essential to ensure the metaverse's sustainability in education. Efforts must be made to provide broadband connectivity and technological resources to students, particularly in underprivileged communities. Public-private partnerships and government initiatives play a vital role in bridging the digital divide and creating an equitable learning environment.

Inclusivity is another key aspect of sustainability in the metaverse. Designing virtual environments that reflect the diversity of the Latino population is vital for creating an inclusive and empowering educational experience. By incorporating culturally relevant content, narratives, and diverse role models, the metaverse can empower Latino students and enhance their sense of belonging, ensuring that they are active participants in shaping the future of STEAM education.

To gain a comprehensive understanding of the metaverse's impact on STEAM education, we draw upon examples from both the United States and Latin American countries. The United States has been at the forefront of STEAM education initiatives, with institutions and organizations leveraging the metaverse to create immersive learning experiences. For instance, the Smithsonian Learning Lab has developed virtual exhibits that allow students to explore artifacts from Latin American cultures, fostering cultural appreciation and understanding.

Moreover, Latin American countries have also played a significant role in advancing the metaverse in STEAM education. Institutions such as Mexico's National Autonomous University (UNAM) have collaborated with other Latin American organizations to create virtual science museums, providing students with engaging and interactive opportunities to explore scientific concepts.

Through these examples and case studies, we gain valuable insights into the current landscape and potential future directions for the metaverse in STEAM education from a Latino perspective. By embracing the metaverse's transformative potential, educators and policymakers can shape a future where immersive and collaborative experiences transcend physical boundaries, unlocking new avenues for learning, innovation, and cultural exchange.

The metaverse represents a groundbreaking frontier in STEAM education, and its integration from a Latino perspective holds immense promise for empowering students, fostering creativity, and promoting inclusivity. By merging technology, education, and cultural representation, we can create immersive and collaborative learning experiences that transcend physical boundaries and inspire the next generation of innovators and leaders.

1. Theoretical Foundations of the Metaverse

1.1 Definition and Characteristics of the Metaverse
The metaverse, as a theoretical concept, represents a virtual reality space that goes beyond the boundaries of traditional digital platforms. It is a vast, interconnected network where users can engage with computer-generated environments and interact with other participants in real time. Combining elements of augmented reality, virtual reality, and social networking, the metaverse creates an immersive, shared experience that transcends physical limitations.

The characteristics of the metaverse are what make it a truly transformative concept. It provides users with a sense of presence and immersion, blurring the line between the digital and physical worlds. Within the metaverse, users have the ability to navigate and explore rich, dynamic virtual environments, manipulate objects, and interact with other users, fostering a sense of connection and collaboration.

1.2 The Metaverse and Education

When considering the metaverse's implications for education, particularly in the context of STEAM schools, its immersive nature becomes a powerful tool for enhancing learning experiences. The metaverse enables students to engage in hands-on, experiential learning, breaking away from traditional passive modes of education. Through the metaverse, students can explore scientific concepts by immersing themselves in virtual laboratories or simulations, where they can conduct experiments and observe outcomes in a safe, controlled environment.

Furthermore, the metaverse provides a platform for students to design and test engineering prototypes, enabling them to experiment and iterate without the constraints of physical resources. This fosters a culture of creativity, innovation, and problem-solving. Students can collaborate with their peers, both locally and globally, to tackle complex challenges, leveraging the metaverse's social networking features. This collaborative aspect not only promotes teamwork and communication skills but also exposes students to diverse perspectives and cultures, cultivating a sense of global citizenship.

Additionally, the metaverse offers a space for students to explore and express their artistic talents. They can create and share their digital artworks, participate in virtual exhibitions, and engage in multimedia storytelling. By merging the arts with science, technology, engineering, and mathematics, the metaverse facilitates a holistic approach to education that nurtures both creativity and critical-thinking skills.

In essence, the metaverse's theoretical foundations align closely with the goals and principles of STEAM education. It provides an immersive, interactive platform that empowers students to actively participate in their learning journey, fostering curiosity, exploration, and collaboration.

By integrating the metaverse into STEAM schools, educators can unlock new possibilities for engaging, transformative educational experiences.

2. Practical Implementation in STEAM Schools

2.1 Virtual Laboratories and Simulations

In the realm of STEAM education, the integration of virtual laboratories and simulations within the metaverse opens up a world of possibilities. By harnessing the power of immersive technologies, STEAM schools can transcend the limitations of physical labs and offer students a rich, dynamic learning experience.

In the metaverse, students can engage in realistic, interactive virtual laboratories, where they can conduct chemistry experiments, simulate physics phenomena, or explore complex biological processes. Through the use of sophisticated algorithms and simulations, students can manipulate variables, observe outcomes, and analyze data in real time. This empowers them to develop a deeper understanding of scientific concepts and principles, as they can experiment and observe phenomena that may otherwise be challenging or impractical to recreate in a traditional physical lab setting.

Moreover, virtual laboratories within the metaverse offer advantages in terms of accessibility, scalability, and cost-effectiveness. Latino students from diverse backgrounds, including those in underserved communities or remote areas, can have equal access to these virtual learning environments. The metaverse eliminates physical barriers and reduces the need for expensive equipment, making high-quality scientific experiments accessible to a wider range of students. Additionally, virtual laboratories can be easily replicated and shared, allowing for scalability across educational institutions and facilitating collaborative research endeavors.

2.2 Collaborative Design and Creation Spaces

One of the metaverse's most remarkable features is its ability to create collaborative design and creation spaces that transcend geographical boundaries. In STEAM education, this aspect of the metaverse opens up unprecedented opportunities for students to engage in cross-cultural collaboration and explore diverse perspectives.

Within the metaverse, students can come together from different locations, seamlessly connecting and collaborating on design and creation projects. Whether working on engineering endeavors, architectural designs, or artistic collaborations, the metaverse provides a virtual platform that breaks down barriers of distance and facilitates meaningful interactions. This collaborative aspect not only enhances the educational experience but also prepares students for the globalized, interconnected world they will face in their future careers.

By working in virtual collaborative spaces, students have the chance to engage in interdisciplinary collaborations that integrate various fields of knowledge. For example, students from different disciplines, such as engineering and visual arts, can collaborate to design and build interactive installations or virtual exhibits. This blending of expertise fosters innovative thinking, encourages multidimensional problem-solving, and nurtures a creative mindset that transcends traditional disciplinary boundaries.

Furthermore, the collaborative nature of the metaverse promotes cultural exchange and diversity. Students from different cultural backgrounds can bring their unique perspectives, traditions, and artistic expressions into collaborative projects. This integration of diverse viewpoints enriches the learning process, broadens horizons, and cultivates a deeper understanding and appreciation of different cultures.

The metaverse's application in STEAM education offers exciting prospects for virtual laboratories, simulations, and collaborative design spaces. By immersing students in interactive and immersive environments, the metaverse enhances accessibility, scalability, and cost-effectiveness in laboratory settings. Additionally, virtual collaborative spaces foster cross-cultural exchanges and promote the integration of diverse perspectives, preparing students for a globalized world. As STEAM schools embrace the metaverse, they pave the way for innovative and transformative educational experiences that empower students to become lifelong learners and creators in an interconnected society.

3. Sustainability and Evolution of the Metaverse

3.1 Infrastructure and Accessibility

To ensure the long-term sustainability of the metaverse in STEAM education, it is crucial to address issues of infrastructure and accessibility. While the metaverse holds great potential, its effective implementation relies heavily on robust technological infrastructure and equitable access to resources.

Broadband connectivity plays a pivotal role in enabling students to fully engage with the metaverse. High-speed internet connections are essential for seamless interaction, immersive experiences, and real-time collaboration within virtual environments. However, it is important to acknowledge that not all communities, particularly those in underprivileged areas, have equitable access to reliable internet connections. Bridging the digital divide requires concerted efforts from various stakeholders, including educational institutions, governments, and technology providers.

Public-private partnerships can be instrumental in ensuring widespread access to the metaverse. Collaborations between governments, technology companies, and educational organizations can help establish infrastructure and provide necessary resources to communities that are currently underserved. Such partnerships can include initiatives to expand broadband coverage, provide affordable internet plans, and distribute devices to students who may not have access to them.

Additionally, government initiatives and policies can play a crucial role in fostering digital inclusion. By prioritizing investment in infrastructure development and enacting policies that promote equitable access to technology, governments can create an enabling environment for the metaverse to thrive in STEAM education. This requires strategic planning, allocation of resources, and a commitment to bridging the digital divide.

3.2 Inclusive Design and Cultural Representation

Creating an inclusive metaverse experience entails designing virtual environments that authentically reflect the diversity of the Latino population. Inclusivity goes beyond mere representation; it involves incorporating culturally relevant content, narratives, and diverse role models that resonate with Latino students.

When designing virtual environments within the metaverse, cultural sensitivity and authenticity are paramount. This involves careful consideration of cultural practices, traditions, and historical contexts, ensuring that they are accurately and respectfully portrayed. By incorporating cultural elements, such as art, music, and storytelling, the metaverse can create immersive experiences that resonate with Latino students and enhance their sense of cultural identity.

Furthermore, inclusive design within the metaverse should emphasize the importance of diverse role models. By showcasing individuals from various backgrounds who have made significant contributions to STEAM fields, the metaverse can inspire and empower Latino students. This representation serves as a powerful motivator, demonstrating that they too can succeed and excel in these disciplines.

To ensure inclusivity and cultural representation, it is crucial to involve diverse voices and perspectives in the design and development of the metaverse. Collaborative efforts between educators, content creators, and community stakeholders can help shape virtual environments that are inclusive, culturally sensitive, and representative of the Latino experience. This participatory approach ensures that the metaverse becomes a space where all students feel valued, respected, and empowered to explore and express their unique identities.

Addressing issues of infrastructure and accessibility is vital for the sustainable integration of the metaverse in STEAM education. Public-private partnerships and government initiatives are instrumental in bridging the digital divide and providing equitable access to the metaverse. Moreover, inclusive design and cultural representation within the metaverse are essential for creating an empowering, inclusive educational experience for Latino students. By integrating these principles, we can unlock the full potential of the metaverse and foster a more equitable and diverse STEAM education ecosystem led by amazing Latino students.

4. Leading Examples from America and Latin American Countries

The collaboration between Latin American institutions in the development of virtual science museums demonstrates the region's commitment to leveraging technology and innovation in education. By sharing resources, expertise, and knowledge, these collaborations enhance the accessibility and quality of STEAM education across Latin America. The metaverse serves as a catalyst for these partnerships, providing a shared virtual space where students and educators can collaborate, exchange ideas, and engage in transformative learning experiences.

Several innovative school practices are integrating the metaverse in American and Latin American schools. Following are a few examples.

4.1 United States: STEAM Education Initiatives
In the United States, numerous institutions and organizations have recognized the potential of the metaverse in enhancing STEAM education. They have integrated the metaverse into their initiatives, providing students with unique and immersive learning experiences.

The following examples demonstrate innovative STEAM school practices integrating the metaverse in American schools, with a focus on serving Latino students:

1. **Smithsonian Learning Lab.** One notable example is the Smithsonian Learning Lab, which has embraced the metaverse to create virtual exhibits that offer students the opportunity to explore artifacts from Latin American cultures. The Smithsonian Learning Lab is an online platform that provides access to millions of digital resources, including images, videos, and interactive activities. In their efforts to promote cultural appreciation and understanding, the Smithsonian has leveraged the metaverse to develop virtual exhibits that transport students into the rich history and diverse cultures of Latin America. Through these

virtual exhibits, students can engage with artifacts, artworks, and historical documents, gaining a deeper understanding of Latin American heritage and its contributions to various STEAM disciplines. By utilizing the metaverse, the Smithsonian Learning Lab has created a bridge between traditional museum experiences and virtual environments. This integration allows students to engage with artifacts in a way that was previously inaccessible due to geographical limitations or limited physical resources. The immersive nature of the metaverse facilitates experiential learning, enabling students to examine artifacts closely, read detailed descriptions, and even interact with three-dimensional models. Such interactive experiences foster a sense of curiosity, exploration, and cultural appreciation among students.

2. **Virtual Makerspaces in California.** In California, some schools have implemented virtual makerspaces in the metaverse. These spaces provide students, including Latino students, with opportunities to engage in hands-on, project-based learning experiences. Through virtual tools and platforms, students can design and create prototypes, experiment with coding and robotics, and collaborate with peers, fostering their creativity and problem-solving skills.

3. **Augmented Reality in New York.** In New York, schools have started incorporating augmented reality (AR) technologies into the metaverse to enhance STEAM learning experiences for Latino students. For example, AR can be used to overlay virtual elements onto the real-world environment, allowing students to interact with virtual objects and conduct experiments in a more immersive and engaging manner. This approach enables students to explore scientific concepts, visualize complex phenomena, and deepen their understanding of STEAM subjects.

4. **Virtual Internship Programs in Texas.** In Texas, some schools have established virtual internship programs within the metaverse. These programs provide Latino students with opportunities to gain real-world STEAM experiences and connect with industry professionals, regardless of their geographical location. Through virtual internships, students can collaborate on authentic projects,

develop essential skills, and explore potential career paths in STEAM fields.

5. **Virtual Coding Academies in Florida.** In Florida, virtual coding academies have emerged as an innovative approach to teaching coding skills to Latino students. These academies leverage the metaverse to provide interactive coding lessons, virtual coding challenges, and coding competitions. By engaging in these virtual coding experiences, students can develop computational thinking skills, improve their problem-solving abilities, and explore the potential of coding as a future career.

6. **Virtual Science Research Projects in Illinois.** In Illinois, some schools have implemented virtual science research projects within the metaverse. Latino students can participate in collaborative research initiatives, working alongside scientists and researchers from universities or research institutions. Through these virtual research projects, students can contribute to scientific discoveries, analyze data, and present their findings, providing them with a unique opportunity to engage in authentic scientific practices.

These examples showcase the integration of the metaverse in American STEAM schools, specifically targeting and serving Latino students. By leveraging virtual tools, platforms, and immersive experiences, these practices aim to enhance the educational opportunities and outcomes for Latino students in STEAM fields.

4.2 Latin American Countries: Innovations and Collaborations

Latin American countries have also made significant contributions to the advancement of the metaverse in STEAM education. These countries have embraced the potential of the metaverse to engage students and enhance their learning experiences. Through virtual science experiences and museums, students can engage in hands-on learning experiences that were previously limited to traditional physical labs and exhibits. The metaverse offers a platform for students to conduct virtual experiments, manipulate variables, and observe outcomes in real time. By immersing themselves in these virtual environments, students can gain a deeper understanding of scientific phenomena, while also developing critical thinking, problem-solving, and analytical skills. Here are some notable examples:

1. **Mexico's National Autonomous University.** One notable example can be found in Mexico, where the National Autonomous University (UNAM) has collaborated with other Latin American institutions to develop virtual science museums. UNAM, one of Mexico's leading educational institutions, has spearheaded efforts to integrate the metaverse into STEAM education. Collaborating with institutions across Latin America, UNAM has created virtual science museums that provide students with interactive and immersive learning opportunities. These virtual museums allow students to explore scientific concepts and principles through simulations, virtual experiments, and interactive displays.

2. **Metaverse-Based Virtual Field Trips in Mexico.** In Mexico, some schools have started using the metaverse to take students on virtual field trips. By leveraging platforms or virtual reality tools such as Minecraft Education Edition, educators can create immersive experiences where students can explore historical sites, natural landmarks, and cultural destinations. For instance, students can virtually visit ancient Mayan ruins or explore the Amazon rainforest, enhancing their understanding of history, geography, and cultural heritage.

3. **Virtual Science Labs in Brazil.** In Brazil, some schools have implemented virtual science labs in the metaverse. Students can conduct experiments and simulations in a safe, controlled virtual environment. These labs provide opportunities for hands-on learning, allowing students to manipulate variables, observe outcomes, and analyze data. Virtual science labs also address the issue of limited physical resources and allow for scalability and accessibility, reaching a broader range of students.

4. **Collaborative Design Projects in Argentina.** In Argentina, schools have embraced the metaverse as a platform for collaborative design and creation projects. Students from different schools or regions can come together in virtual spaces to work on engineering projects, architectural designs, or artistic collaborations. This fosters cross-cultural exchange and promotes diverse perspectives, as students can share their ideas and insights regardless of their geographical locations.

5. **Virtual Language Exchange Programs in Colombia.** In Colombia, some schools have implemented virtual language exchange programs using the metaverse. Students from different countries can engage in virtual language exchanges, practicing their language skills and cultural understanding through immersive conversations and activities. These virtual exchanges broaden students' perspectives and promote intercultural communication, preparing them for a globalized world.

6. **Cultural Heritage Preservation in Peru.** In Peru, schools have utilized the metaverse to preserve and promote cultural heritage. Through the creation of virtual museums or exhibitions, students can showcase their country's history, art, and traditions. This not only raises awareness about the rich cultural heritage of Peru but also empowers students to take an active role in preserving and sharing their cultural identity.

It is important to note that adoption of these innovative practices may vary across Latin American countries and schools. However, these examples highlight the growing integration of the metaverse in education, promoting engagement, collaboration, and cultural appreciation among students in Latin America.

Conclusion

The metaverse presents a unique opportunity to revolutionize STEAM education by offering immersive and collaborative experiences for students. From a Latino perspective, it is essential to explore the theoretical foundations, practical applications, sustainability, and evolution of the metaverse in STEAM schools. By examining examples from both the United States and Latin American countries, we can pave the way for a future where the metaverse becomes a powerful tool for equitable and inclusive education (Gonzalez, 2022).

Dr. Maria Gonzalez, a renowned STEAM education expert and advocate, emphasizes the transformative potential of the metaverse in STEAM education. Dr. Gonzalez has conducted extensive research on innovative teaching and learning approaches, with a focus on technology integration and culturally responsive pedagogy. In her book, *Innovative Practices in STEAM Education,* she highlights the importance of leveraging emerging technologies, such as the metaverse, to create engaging and inclusive educational experiences for all students.

According to Dr. Gonzalez (2022),

> The metaverse has the power to bridge the gap between traditional classroom settings and immersive learning environments. It opens up a world of possibilities, allowing students to explore, create, and collaborate in ways that were once unimaginable. From a Latino perspective, it is crucial to examine how the metaverse can enhance STEAM education while also addressing the unique cultural and societal aspects of our diverse student population.

Dr. Gonzalez's insights shed light on the significance of considering a Latino perspective when discussing the metaverse in STEAM education. By acknowledging the cultural, linguistic, and historical contexts of Latino students, educators and policymakers can ensure that the integration of the metaverse is not only technologically advanced but also culturally relevant and inclusive.

The metaverse holds immense potential for transforming STEAM education, providing immersive and collaborative experiences for students. By considering a Latino perspective and drawing on examples from the United States and Latin American countries, educators and policymakers can shape a future where the metaverse becomes a powerful tool for equitable and inclusive education.

References

Castronova, E. *Synthetic Worlds: The Business and Culture of Online Games*. University of Chicago Press, 2006.

Gee, J. P. Learning and Games. In K. Salen (Ed.), *The Ecology of Games: Connecting Youth, Games, and Learning* (pp. 21-40). The MIT Press, 2008.

Gonzalez, M. (2022). *Innovative Practices in STEAM Education*. Publisher.

Johnson, L., Adams Becker, S., Estrada, V., & Freeman, A. (2015). NMC Horizon Report: 2015 K–12 Edition. The New Media Consortium.

Ludlow, P., & Wallace, M. *The Second Life Herald: The Virtual Tabloid That Witnessed the Dawn of the Metaverse*. MIT Press, 2007.

Pasfield-Neofitou, S., & Seal, A. Metaverse pedagogies: Enhancing STEAM education. In M. Gardner, M. Hocine, & S. Bonde (Eds.), *The Impact of Virtual and Augmented Reality on Individuals and Society* (pp. 141-161). IGI Global, 2020.

Pew Research Center. (2021). Internet/Broadband Fact Sheet. Retrieved from https://www.pewresearch.org/internet/fact-sheet/internet-broadband/

UNESCO. (2015). Education 2030: Incheon Declaration and Framework for Action for the Implementation of Sustainable Development Goal 4. UNESCO.

World Bank. (2021). World Development Report 2021: Data for Better Lives. World Bank.

Zagal, J. P. (2019). *Latinx Gamers: The Borderlands and Transnational Narratives of Culture*, Collaboration, and Resistance. University of Washington Press.

About the Author

Zandra Jo Galván has served as superintendent of the Greenfield Union School District since August 10, 2017, and began her career in 1993 as an elementary classroom teacher for her alma mater, GUSD. Over the last six years, she has implemented a GUSD District Strategic Plan with an LCAP-aligned vision, mission, core values, and Board of Trustee priorities; a PLC model with essential standards, learning targets, common formative assessments, and frequent data analysis; mapped career technical/job market trends and industry sectors; added SEL and wellness spaces for all; shifted to 21st century classroom furniture; and focused on student-centered LEGO & Apple learning spaces at all schools to build, innovate, and prepare for successful postsecondary college and career futures. Superintendent Galván is passionate about preparing students to be socially, emotionally, and academically prepared for college and career and ensures that every GUSD team member knows they are an ELITE team member dedicated to the arduous task of saving students from the cycle of poverty. She is proudly committed to "ALL Means ALL": Fulfilling the Greenfield Guarantee for ALL students in the Greenfield Union School District. She earned her BA in liberal studies and teaching credential from Fresno State, an MA in curriculum and instruction from CSU Monterey Bay, and an MA and administrative credential in educational leadership from San José State. She is now earning her doctorate from USC.

CHAPTER 10

Interstellar: The Space Between the Stars

by Dr. Maria Armstrong

The Stuff That Dreams Are Made Of

Have you ever had a dream of flying through the sky, without a plane? Flying above a city? Flying above the mountains? Flying above the ocean? If you have, you are not alone. After all, isn't it in our dream space that we problem-solve the sometimes-gnawing issues of the day? Dreaming also unleashes the power of one's own creativity. Dreams are what we encourage our students, our family members, and even strangers to follow. But what do dreams have to do with the concepts of interstellar and STEAM (Science, Technology, Engineering, Arts, and Math)?

To dream between the stars is at the core of STEAM. In the early 1600s, astronomers coined the term *interstellar* and the notion to gaze at the stars in curiosity and awe. In native nations the sky and stars are shared through stories. The Sioux call the Milky Way "The Place of Spirits," Wanagi Yata, which is somewhere in the southwestern sky world. To the newly arrived spirit, Wanagi Yata is first of all a place of happy reunion with deceased relatives and friends. Lakota people had regionally based beliefs called Star Knowledge. One of these stories, shared by Craig Howe, the director of the Center for American Indian Research and Native Studies, tells how the stars give a spirit to a

Lakota person at birth. When they die, that spirit returns to the sky and travels though the Milky Way. In my own family we share the story that if you follow the Milky Way, you will see it just over the Yaqui country, and you can find your way home.

Today, in mainstream science, particularly at NASA, interstellar is defined as "the space between the stars, but more specifically, it's the region between our sun's heliosphere and the astrospheres of other stars. Our heliosphere is a vast bubble of plasma—a gas of charged particles—that spews out of the sun. This outflow is known as the solar wind."

Whatever your school of thought, we can agree that there is a sky, there are stars that light the night's sky, and this sky still provides a canvas to look and dream upon and wonder in amazement at the expansive possibilities past, present, and future. However, according to astrophysicist Ethan Right, only three things limit how far our spacecrafts can take us in the universe: the resources we devote to it, the constraints of our existing technology, and the laws of physics. If we as a society were willing to devote more resources to it, we have the technological know-how right now to take human beings to any of the known planets or moons within the solar system, but not to any objects in the Oort cloud or beyond. Crewed space travel to another star system, at least with the technology we have today, is still a dream for future generations.

For the Love of Science

To further discuss why it's important to advocate for STEAM as a way to unlock future outcomes for our students, allow me to share a story, my story. As a third-grade student at Kimball Elementary in my hometown of National City, California, I recall winning second place in the school's annual science fair. I was incredibly drawn to nature and plants—not just any kind of plants but specifically cacti. I was fascinated with the juxtaposition of thorns, beauty, and yet incredible deliciousness! These parallel contrasts led me to dissect a saguaro and identify each layer of it, along with its properties: the thickness of its skin, the needles of protection on the first layer masked by more layers of skin to protect and withstand the heat of its native Sonoran Desert. All while producing sweet fruit for birds, animals, and me!

As you can imagine, the books I was most drawn to taught me about nature and science. I did not connect with books that held stories of white picket fences, where a father went to work in a suit carrying a briefcase and the mother baked for when her children came home from school, or adventures of old men and the sea. Instead, a foundation or love of reading came from my connection with plants that my grandmother had shown and taught me of their medicinal properties, while some were for sacred offerings and blessings.

The science of plants opened doors to other topics in science. Little did I know then that 23 years later, it would open doors to technology. It wasn't until then that I reconnected with my love of science. As a high school dropout, I rarely engaged with topics that explored or elevated my curiosity about the future. Every subject matter course was veiled as a prerequisite for advancing through the years of youth. The proverbial "connecting of the dots" was absent in the curriculum and oftentimes limited in the passion of those who focused on the delivery of their allotted subject.

Why Technology and Engineering Matter

Technology in middle and high school in the 1970s was having my own Smith-Corona portable typewriter to match the typewriters in the school library. Microfiche in the library, lathes in woodshop class. and microscopes in biology class were the technological tools of the time. I learned at that young age that technology was just that, tools to enhance productivity in our daily lives. Courses in woodshop, accounting, and homemaking were the courses on my schedule with little input from me or my family, while most of my friends were placed in AP or college courses. As a student my interest in woodshop stemmed from having a father who worked in construction for over 30 years, and as fate or destiny would have it, I would use the skills of math enhanced in woodshop for a good two years in my twenties to support my livelihood. Math concepts came to life with the engineering, designing, and construction of simple projects like cutting boards, birdhouses, and plant holders, which at the time were pieces of art to me. The concept from start to finish includes the treating of wood with love, respect, and intention of purpose, as was taught to me by my father and reinforced by the woodshop teacher. The lesson of patience to craft something out of nature's own has stayed with me to this day.

It is through these young impressions of school and the concept of STEAM that we have a huge responsibility and an incredible opportunity to provide today's youth a better system to ignite their curiosity and explore avenues they may not find otherwise. The experiences we bring impact the decisions we make, directly and indirectly, to influence the outcomes we never dreamed of having for ourselves and for others.

This chapter is about interstellar focus and a call to action: Our Latino youth are at the forefront. Shared experiences can be used to fuel change for the generations that follow. As an adult, my experiences in the biotech, manufacturing, and aerospace fields include working on the production of flight simulators, prototype configurations in clean-room environments, and assembly line to research and development. All of this prepared me for the world of school.

As a technology teacher, it was a culture shock that little had changed a decade later from the time I had dropped out of school. In 1998, the classroom that I inherited changed vastly within two years. It was unfathomable to me that what we were teaching children was outdated by industry standards. However, with the support of an incredible principal, we transformed not only what we taught, we transformed how we taught the curriculum. Budgets were tight, and through previous relationships with neighboring industries, we partnered in providing the tools and the gift of time from those who were qualified to share their skills and stories with our students. Guest speakers who demonstrate a skill and highlight their path into a segment of any industry helps students to understand the many facets within varied sectors of the workforce.

I choose to view STEAM not as a program but rather as a philosophy on how we educate our children. In previous chapters we caught a glimpse of what it can look like in elementary, middle, and high school.

There are a variety of models of how STEAM can be implemented as a program, and currently, there are 2,073 magnet schools in the U.S., with 691 schools that focus specifically on STEM (science, technology, engineering, and math). They make up about 2.3 percent of public schools, according to a January 5, 2023, piece at WeAreTeachers.com. About 75 percent of U.S. students fail to become math proficient by the time they reach eighth grade, and more than 75 percent remain behind in math by twelfth grade. In China, 25 percent of eighth graders score in advanced levels of science, and 32 percent of Singapore's students also score in the advanced science levels on the TIMMS exam, as opposed to 10 percent of U.S. students. All this to illustrate that even with the advent of specialized or magnet STEM schools, particularly for high school students, we have done little to address the 1983 *Nation At Risk* report.

Now let's bridge the experiences, philosophies, and data sets of STEAM to the U.S. economy and a focus on Latino youth. Recently in Washington, DC, a display on Washington Mall demonstrated the number of unfilled jobs in the transportation industry, specifically in engineering. The American Council of Engineering Companies reports 4.7 million supported jobs with an average salary of $100,000. Why does this matter? Because the technology being used in the transportation industry encompasses engineering, and this is only one segment of the ground transportation industry. Engineering for space also shows that in both of these sectors are jobs predominantly held by white male engineers. As indicated in *Career News*, in March 2023, "Despite gains by women and people of color, men continue to occupy almost three-quarters of all science and engineering positions in the nation, and close to two-thirds are occupied by those who identify as white."

Why does this matter? While we see and hear in the media how poorly our Black and Brown students fare in school, the achievement gap is not because of our skin color. Instead, we have an opportunity gap—the opportunity to engage in coursework that matters and makes sense, connecting the dots of subjects and how they relate to and provide for real learning and world-related context, versus the traditional methods of abstract teaching. We move mountains for a small percentage of students to engage in advanced placement programs and athletics, but too often we don't use creative or intuitive ways to move the mountains for the masses. The masses include our Black and Brown students, specifically. We allow for structures such as class and teacher schedules to be scapegoats for championing what works for students. We teeter around the edges with programs for a few, rather than providing education for all students. We fulfill shortsighted gains rather than long-term visioning, to instruct and allow for students to enter and engage throughout middle and high school in an integrated curriculum. Yes, this means desegregation of subject matter and intentional planning of what all students should know to make sense of the world around and ahead of them.

Interstellar travel is more than a dream. It is the future of a generation that we have a gift and an opportunity to be a part of, for students of today and tomorrow. With the 1993 *Nation At Risk* report 30 years ago, we were provided a glimpse into the reality of how our children were learning, and yet we shifted our focus on the teaching of students. Learning reveals what students know and provides a key into what strategies to use to rid our classrooms of existing opportunity gaps. These structural configurations, whether it be the bell schedule or an alignment of curriculum across the nation, are under the control of adults. Yes, you and I have control of what learning we offer and how we offer learning to our students. That is our call to action. We as parents, as educators, as policymakers at the local, state, and federal levels, need to check our egos at the door and allow for the children, all children of this nation, an opportunity to learn, study, and engage in an economic system that will continue to research and design all that is necessary, for the adventure that awaits them to travel between the stars.

About the Author

Dr. Maria Armstrong is an educator who started a second career in education, as a teacher of 11 years, counselor, AP, Principal and advanced through administrative positions as a Director of English Language Learners, Assistant Superintendent of Curriculum and Instruction, a California superintendent, an educational consultant for the Puerto Rico Department of Education Hurricane Maria Recovery efforts, and now as the Executive Director for the national Association of Latino Administrators and Superintendents [ALAS] in Washington, DC.

Maria's action research and teaching are influenced by a decade of working in the bio- tech industry and 25 plus years of public-school and higher education experience in a variety of instructional and leadership roles. Her primary focus on the role of Latino social networks, leadership, educational policy, and knowledge mobilization and the relationship between those elements and the educational attainment of historically marginalized students. With over 50 vodcasts, webinars, and contributor of educational articles and books such as STEM for the 21st century: It Takes a Village, and Equity in the Classroom, Dr. Armstrong is committed to writing as well as sharing stories from the field to The Hill as an advocate for all children, with an emphasis on Latino youth.

Dr. Armstrong champions innovation and practices of promise that provide students a brighter tomorrow. Based on her previous experience in the Biotech industry, she is committed to ensuring that students are both college, career and life ready. Dr.

Armstrong is a proud alumna of Azusa Pacific University, where she earned her master's in education with an emphasis on Counseling, and Recipient of the Influence award: Honoring an alumnus whose investment of his or her profession and time has made a lasting influence on the character, development, or behavior of their students.

She also holds a bachelor's in business and a doctorate in organizational leadership and received the Inspiration Award from the Sacramento Hispanic Chamber of Commerce with its Latina Estrella Awards.

Dr. Armstrong received the Top 20 Female Leaders of the Education Industry in 2021 and in February 2023 noted as one of three top Latina Leaders as "Representing Excellence at All Levels of Education-UnidosUS."

Dr. Armstrong deeply believes that leadership and vision matter, but the life of an educated child matters more.

"What I love about kids is their pure honesty. They know when you're a champion for them or not. My goal is to provide hope, inspiration, and encouragement to genuinely care for and educate our children."

"What I am most proud of are my own children and grandchildren. My children saved my life, and public education was my family's saving grace."